PRAISE FOR

## *for* JOSHUA

"I hope that when Joshua does eventually read this book, he has the maturity to appreciate his father's act of bravery, and to learn from it. For the rest of us, *For Joshua* is a fascinating and moving portrayal of one man's search for his heritage, his true place in the world, and in the process, his discovery of himself."

—*Hamilton Spectator*

"The writer who did not know himself—and who blamed 'the white man' for his troubles—has become the man who understands how things happened and who resolves to go forward. This well-written and perceptive book shows that it is possible for aboriginal people—for any person—to get back from there to here."

—*Quill & Quire*

"Real . . . honest . . . Those familiar with the native community will be nodding their heads in understanding. Those not very familiar will get a 228-page snapshot of the darker side . . . a darker side with a light in the distance that Wagamese seems to be constantly trying to find. . . . Wagamese writes his story with the spirit of a poet. In particular, the presence of Charles Bukowski can be seen coaching his prose from the sidelines as Wagamese revisits old haunts."

—Drew Hayden Taylor, *The Globe and Mail*

"Paper-cut sharp, linear slices of a life lived in omission. . . . It's a deep, dark path Wagamese sets out on, one he admits is an ongoing process, a circle he learns more from with each revolution."

—*Georgia Straight*

"Graceful and reverberating. . . . A harrowing life story but also a ceremony, a gathering of traditional knowledge, and a love letter across the generations, *For Joshua* is a book we need, a book we can all treasure."

—Warren Cariou, author of *Lake of the Prairies*

An absence of identity, and the struggle to attain it, lies at the heart of this powerful autobiography, in which Wagamese lays bare a disastrous life. . . . Dark and disturbing, still [Joshua] brims with emotion, touching chords of sympathy, even when empathy fails."

—*The StarPhoenix* (Saskatoon)

ALSO BY RICHARD WAGAMESE

*Keeper 'n Me*

*A Quality of Light*

# *for* JOSHUA

AN OJIBWAY FATHER TEACHES HIS SON

# RICHARD WAGAMESE

ANCHOR CANADA

National Library of Canada Cataloguing in Publication

Wagamese, Richard
For Joshua : an Ojibway father teaches his son / Richard Wagamese.

ISBN 0-385-65953-9

1. Wagamese, Richard--Correspondence.  2. Authors, Canadian
(English)--Correspondence.  3. Wagamese, Richard--Alcohol use.
4. Ojibwa Indians.  I. Title.

PS8595.A363Z547 2003      C813'.54      C2003-900638-7
PR9199.3.W316Z497 2003

Cover image: © Brad Wilson/Photonica
Cover and text design: Kelly Hill
Printed and bound in Canada

Published in Canada by
Anchor Canada, a division of
Random House of Canada Limited

Visit Random House of Canada Limited's website: www.randomhouse.ca

TRANS 10 9 8 7 6 5 4 3 2

I was created to be *Anishanabe-niini*—Indian Man. Thus, I was born Ojibway. I emerged onto Mother Earth as a human being gifted with this identity—male Ojibway human being. Since 1955, learning to be who I was created to be has been my journey, my trial, my ongoing process of creation.

This thing we call Native, Indian, First Nations, Aboriginal, Indigenous, or Original Peoples cannot be found in any one place. It is a cosmology, a belief, a way of being, unconstrained by geography, politics or even time itself. It is too immense to be contained in one simple definition. Only with the utmost simplification can one say, "*This is what it means to be Indian.*"

The lives of Native people in Canada are ones of endless toil, frustration and heartache. This they have borne with great good humour, grace, and dignity. To say that I am one of them is my greatest pride.

But I am only one—and this is but the story of one Native life, as experienced against the flux and flow of

Canada over forty-six years. If it teaches, that is grace. If it evokes empathy, that is blessing. Should it enable one person, Native or not, to step forward towards who they were created to be, that would be reward enough for one Native life.

R.W.

*for* JOSHUA

*for* JOSHUA

Once there was a lonely little boy. He had no idea where he belonged in the world. The boy had no knowledge about where his family was or where he'd come from. So he began to dream. He imagined a glorious life with a mother and father, sisters and brothers, grandfathers and grandmothers. He put his dreams down on paper and filled the pages with drawings, stories, poems, and songs of the people he missed so much but could not remember. But he always awoke, the stories and poems always ended, and the songs faded off into the night.

As he grew, the boy carried this emptiness around inside him. Everywhere he went, it was his constant companion. Many people took turns caring for the boy, and many people tried to fill that hole, but no one ever could. Through all the homes he drifted the boy began to realize that all that ever really changed about him were his clothes.

One day, the people around him said that he was old enough to go and find *there*. It was a magical place, this place called *there*, because everyone got to choose where *there* would be for them.

But finding *there* was difficult. The boy took many roads, many turns, many long lonely journeys trying to find it. He grew older. He lived in many places and with many different people. But inside himself he was still a lonely little boy who could only ever dream dreams, create stories and poems and songs about the kingdom of *there*.

Then one day he met a kind, gentle old man on one of the twisted, narrow roads he was travelling. This old man had been everywhere and seen many things. He was wise and liked the young man very much. As they sat together by the side of that long, narrow road, the old man began to tell him stories about all of his travels, and especially about how good it felt to return from those journeys.

"What is *return?*" the young man asked.

"Why, it's to get back to where you started, where you belong," the old man said.

"What does it mean to *belong?*"

The old man smiled kindly and said, "To *belong* is to feel right. It's a place where everything fits."

"How do you get there?" the young man asked.

"Well, getting anywhere means you have to make a journey. But on this journey, to find where you belong, you really only have to travel one direction," the old man said.

"What direction is that?"

"The toughest direction of all," the old man said. "You have to travel inside yourself, not down long, narrow roads like this one."

"Does it hurt?" the young man asked.

"Sometimes. But anyone who makes that journey finds out that no matter how hard the journey is, getting there is the biggest comfort of all."

The young man thought about the old man's words. They were mysterious and strange. In fact, they weren't answers to his questions at all, just more and more questions lined up one behind the other as far as he allowed his mind to wander. But there was something in the gentle way the old man had of talking that made him feel safe—a trust that everything he said was true. Even if he couldn't understand it all.

"Can I get there from here?" he asked finally.

The old man smiled at him and patted him on the shoulder. "Here is the only place you *can* start from."

I was that lonely little boy, Joshua, and I was the lonely young man who tried so hard to belong. Like him, I have travelled a lot of hard roads searching for the one thing that would allow me to feel safe, secure, and welcome. Some of them led to prison, poverty, drunkenness, drugs, depression, isolation, and thoughts of suicide. But many were glorious roads to travel—the ones that led to sobriety, friendship, music, writing, and the empowering traditional ways of the Ojibway people to whom you and I belong.

There were many teachers on those roads. Always there was someone somewhere who offered things meant to teach me how to see the world and my place in it. But like most of us, I only ever trusted my mind—and my mind always needed proof. The sad thing is that when you spend all your time in a search for proof, you miss the magic of the journey, and I was on those roads a long, long time before I learned the most important lesson of all: that the journey is the teaching, and the proof of the truthfulness of all things comes secretly, mysteriously, when you find yourself smiling when you used to cry, and staying staunchly in place when you used to run away.

I spent many years afraid of the questions. I was afraid of the questions because I was afraid of the answers, and that fear kept me on narrow, twisted roads deep into my life.

My greatest fear was that after the search, after the most arduous of journeys, I would discover, at the end, a me I didn't like, the me that I was always convinced I was: an unlovable, inadequate, weak, unworthy human being. And at that point of discovery I would be alone. Alone with myself. Alone with my fears. Alone with the one person I had spent so much time and energy trying to run away from.

When I was scared I ran, from darkness to darkness. But flight is futile when the bitterest pain is the memory of the people that get left behind. The innocent ones bearing the hurts and disappointments of our leaving, standing by the wayside watching as we disappear down another sullen highway. They never really understand departure. They can't. Because we are incapable of explanation. We only know that we need to move on, desperate gypsies seeking the solace of flight, the vague, lingering hope that geography, in some way, might save us.

You are one of the innocent ones. You are six years old at this writing and because of the choices I made during the part of my journey since your birth, we are not together. I chose drink and isolation to deal with my pain, my fear, and the resultant overwhelming sense of inadequacy, and the effect of those choices is a life where son and father cannot live together—perhaps not ever.

Today the ache of your absence is hard.

Because I was there at the very moment you entered the world. I stood beside your mother when she delivered you. I received you from the nurse and held you, afraid that I might press too hard and hurt you, or not press firmly enough and let you tumble from my grasp. I held you like the treasure that you are. When I looked at you that April morning I found myself grateful for a Creator that could fashion such a magnificent being, such a beautiful boy, such a gift to me. Your arrival filled my heart with joy, and it was so great it spilled over into the empty side of my chest and made me more—bigger, stronger, more alive. I didn't want to give you back to them when they asked to weigh and measure you. I didn't want to give you back because I didn't want to surrender that feeling your arrival had created in me.

For a time I felt like a father. I'd never been one before and learning to change your diapers, rock you to sleep, feed you, and get you to giggle were private joys that I still carry in my heart. They are my pocket treasures and even though they've been worn smooth from handling over the years, it's comforting to know that they are there when I need them.

You and I would wander along Danforth Avenue in Toronto. I carried you on my chest in your carrier and talked to you about where we were going and what we were seeing. We got a lot of strange looks from the people we passed because I was not ashamed to talk to you out loud, laugh, and coax you to make some happy noise. There was a bookstore we'd go into almost every day and I'd read to you from my favourite volumes. We'd go to a small park and I'd sing to you as we swung slowly back and forth on the swing set in the playground. You used to love that. And as we moved together through the great, grand noise that is Toronto I heard nothing but you and felt nothing but the warmth of your body nestled against mine. I can't enter that city now without a feeling of incredible loss or joy for you.

Drinking is why we are separated.

That's the plain and simple truth of it. I was a drunk and never faced the truth about myself—that I was a drunk. Booze owned me. I offered myself to it when I was a young man and it was only too glad to accept me into the ranks of its worshippers, the ones who are willing to pay with everything for one more round. I drank because it made things disappear. Things like shyness, inadequacy, low self-worth—and fear. I drank out of the fears I'd carried all my life, the fears I could never tell anyone about, the fears that ate away at me constantly, even in the happiest moments of my life, and your mother did the only thing that she knew to do and that was to take you away where you could be safe. I don't blame her for that. I'm thankful in fact. I drank on and off, like I'd done all my life, and your mother grew tired of my constantly returning to the bottle. She refused to let me see you. When I finally got sober I knew I had responsibilities, but by then we'd been apart more than two years. This book is my way of living up to some of that responsibility.

As Ojibway men, we are taught that it is the father's responsibility to introduce our children to the world. In the old traditional way, an Ojibway man would take his child with him on his journeys along the trap lines, on hunting trips, fishing or just on long rambles across the land. The father would point out the things he saw on those outings and tell his child the name of everything he saw, explain its function, its place in Creation. Even though the child was an infant and incapable of understanding, the traditional man would do this thing. He would explain that the child was a brother or a sister to everything and that there was no need to fear anything because they were all relations.

The father would perform this ritual so the child would feel that it *belonged*. He would do this so that the child would never feel separated from the heartbeat of Mother Earth. So that children would always feel that heartbeat in the soles of their feet. He would do it so that kinship was one of the first teachings the child received. The father would do this to honour the ancient ways that taught us that we are all, animate and inanimate alike, living on the one pure breath with which the Creator gave life to the Universe.

And he did it for himself.

He performed this task so he could learn that devotion is a duty driven by love, one which has its beginnings in the earliest stage of life, and that teaching, preparing a child for the world, begins then as well.

This book is my way of performing that traditional duty. I do not know if or when we will be together. Because of the way I chose to live my life, the price we've paid is separation. I am neither a hunter nor a trapper. I am not a teacher, healer, drummer, singer, or dancer. Nor am I a wise man. But I offer this book as a means of fulfilling that traditional responsibility. I want to introduce you to the world, to Creation, to the landscape I have walked, to some of the people who have shaped my life. All I have to offer is all that I have seen, all the varied people I became, and maybe you will glean from all of it an idea of the father that my life and my choices have denied you.

# INITIATION

I was thirty-two years old the summer I met John. I remember feeling like a much older man throughout that spring and early summer. I was weary from the effort of trying to hang on. I'd been hanging on for a long time by then. Meeting him was like the feeling you get after a long portage, when you see open water again and feel the relief and the expectation of a better journey.

My first marriage had ended two years before, and I felt like a failure. I felt there was nothing I could do, nothing I could build that would last, nothing I could choose that would bring me happiness. So I'd spent two years trying to get as drunk as I could so that I could forget. Two years choosing numbness over feeling. Isolation over the tug of life. When you give yourself up to it the way I did those two years, liquor becomes something you immerse yourself in, not just something you drink. And when you drink, you drink down.

There's a belief in the beginning, with that first swallow, that you're elevating yourself somehow, lifting yourself above the problems, the pain, confusion, and fear that live in your belly. You drink to drown these things, to fill your belly with courage, your mind with painless thoughts, your spirit with abandon—and you believe you raise yourself above it all with one liquid rush. But you always drink down. Because when you give yourself to alcohol, in the complete way that you do to love, sometimes, or to God, you surrender the right to innocence, to humanity, and you forfeit the permission to enter those glittering palaces filled with the laughing, energetic folk you crave to be among. Instead, you learn to pay the most expensive dues in the world and join the club of drunks and sots who drink the way you do, or preferably even worse.

You drink your way down to dank, dark rooms where conversation is a mumbled order for one more round, and downward further to one-room mansions where a jug is the only furniture needed, and then downward to the riverbanks, back alleys, and isolated places where solitude is a virtue. You drink down from languid sips from splendid glasses to furtive gulping from cheap bottles. You drink down from Scotch and vodka to mouthwash, shaving lotion, rubbing alcohol, and Lysol. You drink down to the point where you forget everything about being human and you learn to live for the burn in the belly that says you can last one more hour, one more jug, maybe one more day.

I drank like that for years. I had to, because I knew no other way around the feelings churning in my gut. I always drank down to where I couldn't drink any more, then endured the rigours, the terror, of sobering up and re-entering the world. Because I was a binge drinker I had extended periods when I didn't drink, and during those times hope would rise in me that maybe this time I could avoid the seemingly inevitable collision with myself that always ended in that crazy downward spiral. In those times I worked, fell in love, played and lived almost like normal people do. Except for the fact that I never changed anything, never sought a re-evaluation of my attitude towards life. When the fear returned—as it always did, sometimes after a year or more, sometimes after a few months—I drank because it was the only way I knew. It was all I had ever learned about coping.

Sometimes I sought sobriety with the same desperation

with which I sought a drink. When I did, I play-acted at liking it. I gave memorable performances as a journalist, radio host, husband, lover, and friend. I could have earned an Oscar if there were a category for Best Performance by an Actor in a Limited Role, because I never learned to be among people the way others do. Life, the way I lived it, had never prepared me for that. Life as a drunk had taught me that reaching out was a pushing away, not a pulling in. Instead, I only ever offered enough to be invited in from my aloneness, then lingered on the edges of the circles I joined. I liked it at the edges because escaping back to alcohol was easier from there. Far easier than when you were immersed in a life. Knee-deep even was too far for me, so I only ever offered up the minimum, the least I could get away with offering of myself to keep from being alone.

But alone is where I always ended up. I never believed that there was anything that could change that, spin my life on its axis and show me a new direction. But I was wrong. I came off a binge in Calgary, sobered up, went to work, and became very deliberate in the choices I made. Deliberate enough to put ten months together without a drink. And that's when I met John.

John had waged his own battle with the bottle. It was a monumental struggle because he had drunk the same way I did, except he had been a daily drinker, one of those who drown themselves in it from sun-up to sunset, until they keel over in defeat or death. John had been defeated and he knew it. He had been sober more than ten years when we met and had become a teacher of the traditional ways of our people. When he met me for the first time he just smiled, shook my hand, and looked at me with a pair of deep brown eyes that seemed to see right into me. He nodded at me and clapped a hand around my shoulders. No words were spoken, but I heard him say a lot in that small gesture. John *knew*. He knew in the intuitive way one desperation drinker knows another—by the history stencilled on our faces, the look that makes us pariahs, outcasts amongst the normal drinkers, but tells us we're with another of the same breed, both when we're drinking and when we're not. He knew about the journeys I had taken, about the search for a right place, about the people, the things, the jobs, the money, and the light that was sparked in me every now and then that I could never keep lit. When he looked at me I felt *known*, and I trusted him.

He was an Ojibway. That helped. Fiftyish, he was tall, lean, with grey hair he kept tied in a long ponytail. He loved to joke and tease gently. His laugh was loud and contagious. When he told a story he was capable of making the world disappear and you would feel lifted up and transported to another world for as long as that tale lasted. He was the first person I'd ever met whom I could describe as disarming—he owned that indescribable knack for scaling the walls that damaged people like me erect around ourselves.

I started to tell John the stories of where I'd been. About the times in my life when I was confused and the many times I was afraid. I told him about the great weight of not knowing where I belonged, or where I was supposed to go in life. I talked about the wandering paths of my exile. I had worked as a tavern waiter, serving beer to longshoremen and the sailors who worked on the shipping lanes of the St. Lawrence River, and as a labourer on construction sites; I had pushed huge sleds filled with raw steel plates around a factory floor, planted trees, levelled railroad tracks, been a radio disc jockey, newspaper reporter, television host and producer, and I had mopped floors. Through all of these jobs I was looking for my place. But I'd never found it.

I tried living in different places: Toronto, Winnipeg, Vancouver, Edmonton, Calgary, Regina, Ottawa, Kenora, Minaki, and a lot of smaller places for brief periods of time. In my younger days I hitchhiked around the country three times, looking for that one place I knew I could feel at peace, whole and content. I saw a lot of Canada, met a lot of people, did a lot of things, but I never found that one place.

But I came close many times. I would be in a place and it would feel right. I would feel *right*. One time it was on a high spire of rock in front of a waterfall in the Rocky Mountains. The cliffs on either side of me dropped away suddenly and the place where I stood was about the size of a tabletop. The water poured over the face of those cliffs about twenty feet in front of my face and there was a mystical feeling of emptiness in that span of twenty feet—an emptiness and a fullness at the same time. I could have stepped off and dropped straight down for hundreds of feet, landing in the swirling waters of turquoise, white, and silver. The mist was like pellets of mercury—icy cold against my face. The mountains were gathered around me like the heads and shoulders of friends, and there was no one else around for miles. It was just me and Creation in all its purity and I felt *right*. I stayed in that spot for hours just absorbing it all, hoping that I could carry some part of it back into the world with me, some part that would let me feel that way wherever I wound up. I couldn't.

Still other times I would be at a play, a concert, a movie, or reading a book somewhere, and I would become so wrapped up in it all, in the sheer joy of experiencing someone's magic spread out before me, that I would feel content and safe. The magic that is creativity would spark a light in me, a light that I found in literature, in the brush strokes of great painters, in music, dance, theatre, and film. When I was lost in that generous spirit, I would drink it all in, hoping that I could carry some part of it back into the world with me, some small part that would allow me to feel that rightness, that security, wherever I wound up. I couldn't.

I tried finding rightness in money, cars, clothes, and all the bright and shiny things of the world. But they were only ever things, and I learned that things fade, get old, fall out of fashion, become uncool, unhip, unspectacular and incapable of giving a feeling of rightness anymore.

I told John all of that. Later, after I saw that he avoided judging me for what I said, and only murmured in agreement or recognition as I spoke, I told him about the booze. We began to talk. Real conversations that dizzied me in the ease with which they emerged from the great silence my life had been until then. In the beginning, these talks weren't big ones. In fact, they made me feel like a little kid again. When you're a kid and you have something you really, really want to say but can't find the words for, you spend a lot of time doodling around in the sand with your toe. With John, at first, I did a lot of doodling around.

But he brought me out, mainly through jokes and stories, and it wasn't long before we were sharing our experiences. I felt like an equal. He allowed me to feel like someone who really mattered. Finally, I was someone who counted, although I had much to learn. John, like any good teacher, made me curious about my feelings, my mysteries, my maps and territories. And like good teachers do, he gave me a compass that led me to explore further than I had before. John did that for me.

He talked to me about the traditions and teachings of our people and how they might just work for me in today's world if I was strong enough to try them. We'd walk through the foothills or the prairies and he would point things out to me and explain how our people understood them. Things like how the prairie grasses symbolized humility, how the mountain symbols painted on a teepee represented faith, why the eagle is such a revered and honoured creature. He talked about the four sacred medicines—sweet grass, tobacco, sage, and cedar—and how they came to be delivered to the people and what they were used for. He explained how much the world had changed in his lifetime and the lifetimes of others of his generation, and how change affected the lives of our people across the country. He explained the nature of traditional life in the tribal times before the settlers came. He told me how important it was for our people to reconnect to those old ways of being so that they might sustain us through even more difficult changes to come. These things and more he explained to me.

When I had questions, which was most of the time, he would explain quietly and humbly what he knew of these things. I never felt he was talking down to me during those conversations. Instead, I felt included, as though these teachings had always belonged to me and I was simply being reminded of them, not lectured to. I loved him for that. When my questions became more pointed, more direct and probing, he figured that I had learned enough to understand at a deeper level and he started to teach me about ceremony.

A ceremony is a very simple thing, I remember him telling me. It's a way of talking to the Creator—*Gitchee Manitou* in the Ojibway language. It's a way to line up your life and how you live it with the simple way of the heart.

Before he explained this to me I had believed that a ceremony was something that would intimidate me, something that would make me feel small, something I should fear. But I learned that a ceremony makes you bigger. It gives you power. It clears your heart, mind, spirit, eyes, ears, and mouth so you can experience the world as it is, not as it's taught to you or as it seems to be sometimes. A ceremony is an act of love, John said. Ojibway ceremonies, when they're done the right way with the right intention, are meant to help you know and understand yourself and your place in the universe.

To get me ready for the arrival of ceremony in my life, John explained the Medicine Wheel. I'd heard of it before, but like so many of the traditional ways of my people, I really had no idea of what it meant. I had some vague, romantic notion that it was an item of regalia to be worn on my chest, a tattoo maybe, or some mysterious object to hang on my wall that would protect me from all kinds of evil things.

"A Medicine Wheel is like a map," he said.

"To lead me where?" I asked.

"To where you live."

"You mean my home?"

"Yes. Where you live. Your insides. The Medicine Wheel acts like a guide to take you there," he replied.

"And why would I need a map for that? Can't I just find the way on my own?"

"Well, we human beings like to think we can," he said. "We all like to believe that we can discover the necessary truths on our own—but we can't. Like it or nor not, we need help, and the Medicine Wheel is one of the greatest tools our people have to help us find our individual truths."

He went on to explain that a Medicine Wheel was a circle divided into four segments, each representing a direction from the physical world, our Mother Earth. The east, the direction of the rising sun, is the place of illumination, and its gift is innocence. The south is the direction that receives the most light from the sun and is the place of growth. Its gift is humility and trust. In the west, the sun sets and is the place where introspection happens in the long night to follow. The gift of the west is honesty. The north is the place of truth. After travelling the other three directions and looking at his life, the traveller who arrives in the north is graced with the gift of wisdom.

"You look at your life, where you've been, what you've done, how you felt about it all. That's how you travel the Medicine Wheel," John said. "The four directions also represent body, emotions, mind, and spirit. When you look back over your life, you look at the four parts of yourself and you gain wisdom. You find your truth."

"I don't get it. Where is this Wheel? Do I have to go somewhere to start making my way around it?" I asked.

"No," he said. "You can use the Wheel and its teachings anywhere. It's inside you where all truth is. You just need to be willing to look for it. If you want to learn about yourself and your life you can walk the Wheel anywhere. And that's exactly what I have in mind for you."

He went on to tell me that it was important for me to

perform a ceremony for myself, one that would enable me to experience what it was like to use the Medicine Wheel and its teachings in my life. Rather than spend an agonizing time talking about these life teachings and how they applied to me, John wanted me to do a ceremony on my own that would make the Medicine Wheel clear to me. I was to gather a yard of white cotton cloth that I would cut into as many small squares as possible. Then, I was to gather some white thread, tobacco, a blanket, and a large canteen. When I had these things I was to let him know. I trusted John, though it felt odd to follow directions without a full explanation. But I believed that a collection of things as seemingly harmless as what he was asking for couldn't bring too fearful a result, so I went along.

"Is there some place you know that's special for you?" he asked when I had gathered all of the materials.

"Yes," I said, without a lot of thought.

There was a hill where I had been going for a month or so to watch sunsets. The hill faced the Rocky Mountains, which were only about twenty miles away. I'd found it by accident one day while driving aimlessly about. Maybe the Ojibway in me, the part that remembered a home territory much like this, with high craggy cliffs and thick bush enveloped in a huge, tangible silence, was attracted to that setting. I don't know. But I do know that it was one of those places that felt right, and I'd returned again and again.

To get to the top I needed to park my car by the side of a gravel road and walk about half a mile around and up to a small copse of trees where there was an outcropping of rock with a ledge from which I could dangle my feet. The drop from that ledge to the road was more than two hundred feet and I had seen eagles and hawks soar between me and the road below. It's an eerie feeling when you see great birds from above, and eerier still when they make their silent passes against a backdrop of coyote howls from the hoodoos and hills all around you. There were bears in that territory, too, though I hadn't seen any during my visits to the hill.

I'd sit there silently and watch the sun fade into the arms of the Rockies and then make my way back down in the gathering darkness, filled with a sense of mystery and a foreign calm that always lessened the closer I got to the city of Calgary again.

"Sounds like it's the right place, then," John said.

We drove out together late one morning. It was summer, and the brilliance of the sun seemed to fill everything we passed with a vibrant energy so that the world was virtually quivering with life. I was vibrating, too, but with a different energy. I was anxious and uncertain and the fact that John didn't talk much on the drive unsettled me further. I sensed that what he was about to ask me to do was a big enough matter that small talk seemed insignificant in the face of it. I felt the knot of apprehension grow in my belly. When we got to the hill we walked to the top of it in the same dense silence.

At the ledge he drew a large circle on the ground with his walking stick. To the west I could see the Rocky Mountains, and I could follow their ragged sweep to the south and north over foothills thick with trees. Eastward, forest, rock, and the huge bowl of the sky hovered over the great plains. The road looked like a pale grey ribbon from that height, and John's car was a small dot of colour at the base of the hill. I felt distant from everything at that moment. When he'd finished inscribing the circle, John told me to sit in it with all my articles.

"This will be your home for the next four days," he said. "You can't step out of this circle for any reason. That meal we ate in town is the last food you'll have for that length of time, and the water you carried in has got to last you through."

I couldn't believe what I was hearing. I would have no fire. I would have nothing to read. My job for the next four days was to sit in that circle and look around at the world. I was to pay strict attention and think about my life.

"Each time you think of something in this world and in your life that you are thankful for, you put tobacco in the cloth and tie it," John instructed. "You look around you and you think. Go back to things, places, people. Try to remember how you felt at certain times in your life. It might be hard—you may cry, you may want to run away—but if you stay and do this thing, you'll find things to be thankful for. You'll learn what it means to have gratitude and you'll make a pouch for each of them."

The pouches were to be tied together with the thread until they formed a long chain. "Then what?" I asked.

"I'll let you know," was all he said.

It seemed like a huge demand. To go without food and shelter was nothing new to me. I'd been homeless on a few occasions in my life and sleeping outdoors was hardly a new experience. But to do so by choice was different. I was suddenly very afraid. The fear came from the idea of being alone and powerless on a hill far removed from the things I'd learned to take for granted in the cities where I'd lived. This was going to just be me, armed with nothing, alone in a world that suddenly seemed untamed and unpredictable, far wilder than it ever had before. I was going to be left alone with myself—and it terrified me.

My mind raced. For the next ninety-six hours I was to be

silent. I could pray aloud if I felt like it, or I could even sing a prayer song, but beyond that I was to remain silent. John told me that the circle I sat in represented life and because of that I needed to be very respectful. I could not kill anything in that circle. If I needed to relieve myself I would have to bury my waste and keep the circle as clean and as pure as possible. The blanket was all the protection I would have. When I grew hungry and uncomfortable I was to pray and let Creation know how I was feeling, but not to ask for anything but the strength to see this ceremony through to its end.

"Are you sure I'm ready for this?" I asked.

"There's only one way to find out," he replied.

"What if something happens? What if some big animal— a bear, or a wolf or something—comes along? What do I do?"

He smiled. "You'll figure that out if it happens."

"You're sure?"

"No. But I'm not the one who has to be," he said with a grin.

"But why? Why is it so important that I put myself through something like this?"

"That's what you'll find out when it's over."

And he walked away.

# I

## INNOCENCE

There are silences in this life that can open up and swallow you whole. You tumble into them, senseless and disoriented. The sudden lack of direction leaves you immobile, foot-stuck, and mute, language suddenly a guttural rasp in the voice box. As I stood in that small copse of trees and watched John make his way back down the hill I wanted to shout that I wasn't ready for this. I needed more time. I didn't know enough. I was scared. But I couldn't find my voice. My throat was dry and coarse with desperation and I took a big swallow of water to ease it. The further away he got, the more alone and isolated I felt and the bigger and emptier the world seemed. When he got into his car and began to pull away I waved my arms at him, but he either didn't see me or was content to leave me on that hill.

I watched his car until it disappeared and then I slumped down to the ground. There was the first chill of an evening breeze and the shadows thrown by the sun were suddenly deeper and longer. It would be evening soon. I looked around at the view that had seemed so friendly before this day but now was heavy with unseen dangers. I was scared. More scared than I could recall ever having been. Without a fire at night I would have no way to prevent anything from coming into that circle. I was afraid to be hungry. Four days without food is a long time and even though we'd had a really big meal before coming to the hill, the thought of being hungry for days frightened me. I was afraid my water would run out. I was fearful of the weather suddenly turning into a summer storm, of lightning, thunder, hail, and cold. I was afraid of insects. But mostly I was afraid that I would fail. Failure at this ceremony would mean that I didn't have what it took to be Indian, to be Ojibway. It would mean that I belonged nowhere, that I would be alone forever.

So I sat there with all my fear and waited. It was beautiful there. The swell and toss of the foothills reminded me of the ocean and I imagined myself on the start of a long voyage. I was a mariner unmoored from the security of the pier and set free on the wild blue abandon that is the sea. It was a good thought.

Before long I settled into the silence. I began to notice that silence wasn't really silence at all. As I sat there looking around, observing, I could hear things I had never heard before, voices of the world that I'd been deaf to, noises and shifts of sound that filled all of that great space around me. There was rustling and cracking coming from the bush below me, the sibilant whisper of wind through the trees, the rattle of gravel spilling down the cliff, and bird calls, squirrel chatter, the lowing of distant cattle, and further away the swish and hum of traffic on the Trans-Canada Highway. The more I strained to hear, the more I began to feel transported, taken back into my life. And I started to recall things, vague memories of times long before in a childhood I'd learned to block off, to refuse to revisit, to mythologize, or lie about completely.

I'd been born in surroundings like this. My life had started amidst the rough and tangle of northwestern Ontario and the sounds I was hearing were the very first sounds I heard when I entered the world in October of 1955.

My family lived a traditional life. The first home I lived in was a canvas tent, deep in the bush across the bay from the small railroad depot at Minaki. I was surrounded by family. Along with my mother and father, sister Jane and brothers Jack and Charles, I lived with aunts and uncles and their children. Our lives were spent hunting, fishing, trapping, gathering berries, smoking fish, and living as Ojibway people had for generations before the settlement of Canada. There was a part of me that remembered all of that. Not in a real way, not with clarity, but more a vague, shadowy recollection, like ghosts moving across a room.

When I closed my eyes that first night the sounds around me stirred those shadows into image and I saw canoes beached in a cove, laden down with furs and traps. The pines back of the small clearing on the shore were thick and green, moving mysteriously into jade, emerald and deeper, into brown and fading to black. There were people moving about in front of canvas tents and in the air was the tang of wood smoke. In my mind's eye this was a happy place, and the family that worked and cavorted around those fires was a happy one engaged in a life, a way of being, that was timeless, unalterable, and real. Tears began to burn the backs of my eyes at the thought of that life and I opened them, shook my head to clear them, and looked about at the world around that hill. That was the life I'd been born to.

I never learned the truth about the reason that life ended for me. Instead I was given different versions of the story from different members of my family, stories that never quite filled the holes within them. I could relate to that. I'd never filled the holes that existed in the story of my life either. As I sat on the hill and looked around I thought that perhaps when you're hurt it's easier to mythologize the past than to explain it, easier to find a source of blame than a source of truth. So I didn't know the real story of how we kids came to be wards of the Children's Aid Society. I did know that alcohol, even then, was a titanic influence and that it was the negative energy of drink that led my brothers and sister and me into the custody of the Children's Aid when I was still a toddler. I can't remember that. Can't recall the moment of separation, or the condition of my life when it happened.

But my sister can. She tells a story about how we were all together in a foster home with the Wright family on Carlton Road outside of Kenora. There was bush all around and, according to her, I really liked it there. Of course, I was far too young to know that I had been stripped from the family tree and that I was a foster child. All that seemed to matter to me was that I was with my brothers and sisters. I followed them everywhere. But they were all old enough to go to school. I stayed at home every day and Jane recalls how I loved to play in the sandbox with the one toy I had—a little red truck with one wheel missing. I played for hours in that sandbox and I loved that little red truck.

One day, she watched out the back window of the school bus as it pulled away. She doesn't know why it was so important for her to look back that day, but she did. She watched me huddled in that sandbox playing with my truck until the bus followed a bend in the road and I slipped out of view. When they got home that night they were told that I had been moved to another foster home.

Jane says she walked outside and stood by that empty sandbox. The little boy she had watched that morning was gone, and all that remained of him was a little red truck with one wheel missing, already partially buried in the sand.

I was gone for more than twenty years and when she told me that story for the first time we hugged each other, held on for a long time, and cried.

My first clear memories are of living in a foster home on the outskirts of Kenora, Ontario. I was four years old.

We lived in a house that was less than a quarter-mile away from the bush and rock I loved even then, and where I played my first games. I had a friend in those days. I'll call him Paul. He and his family were the only Ojibway people in the area. Their house was a small four-room shack with a big black pot-bellied stove in the middle of the centre room. The pipes from that stove went through the walls into each of the other rooms and I used to get a big kick out of seeing his father's long johns and grey wool work socks hung over those pipes to dry. I don't know how many days I stood leaning against the doorjamb listening to his father play guitar and sing. He had a really good voice and his hair was always slicked back like Elvis Presley's. Of course, this was at the end of the 1950s, so he was probably right in style. I'd stand there tapping my feet and wishing that I could make music like that. The songs I heard in that kitchen had titles like "Ring of Fire," "Wabash Cannonball," "Don't Be Cruel," and "Memphis, Tennessee." I loved those songs. I still do. When Paul was ready we'd dash out of the house with music ringing in our ears, on the hunt for big adventures in the northern Ontario bush that started right behind their house.

I'd like to think that Paul and I were good friends. After I was taken away from that foster home years later I never, ever saw him again. But I still remember him. We were both pint-sized Ojibway boys and we both loved to run through the bush. Our games were hunting games. I remember playing hide and seek. It would take me hours sometimes to find him. I know that I too was good at hiding, and that he took just as long to find me.

We loved that bush. We loved that land. We loved it because of the freedom it represented to us. We loved it because it was always there waiting for us and always, always willing to take us just as we were. Naturally, we never used such words to define our love of the woods, and we were too young to understand the connection that exists between an Ojibway and the land. Even if we had known, I don't think we'd have stopped running long enough to consider what it meant to us and the men we would become. We were just boys and all we knew was how much fun it could be prowling about that wide expanse of bush country.

When I close my eyes to recall those days I can still see the patterns the shadows made amongst the trees, the dappled grey faces of the boulders, and the hushed, swaying sound of white water just beyond the ridge. I felt more at home there, hidden behind a thicket of spruce, behind a tumble of boulders, or in the depths of a berry patch than I did in Kenora or the foster home.

Paul felt more at home there, too. His daddy drank too much and often beat him up—beat up his mother and two sisters, too. Thinking back about listening to music in their doorway, I remember seeing bottles on the table, and bits of smashed glass littering the carpet. I guess you're ignorant of those things when you're a kid, or maybe somehow you know by instinct to look past them, to wait with bated breath for the dash to the sunshine, for the chance to lose yourself again in the golden warmth of friendship. But I knew that he always felt safer in the bush. At least out there, he always knew what to expect.

We were like any other Ojibway kids. We were more than a little wild, reckless, careless, and self-centred in our play. Nothing mattered except the total freedom of running through that landscape. Years later, as I looked across the tops of the trees in the foothills, I would recall learning to find rabbits, track foxes and deer, how to recognize fresh bear droppings, and to move extra carefully after that. We learned a lot on our own.

Paul and I both loved fishing. From the first sign of melt in the early spring to the first fall of snow in winter we were mad for fishing. We learned to spear suckers in the spring after Paul saw something similar on television. We made a gill net out of baling twine we had found and we learned how to drive fish along the shallows into the mouth of that net. We learned how to read water for the best places for rod-and-reel fishing.

But most of all we learned to love the land. To love its feel, its smell, its motions, and its stillness. But we had no one to teach us, and everything we discovered we found on our own. The downside was that we never found out that Ojibway boys were supposed to learn to behave like caretakers of the land and all the life it held. We didn't know that simply being Indian by doing an Indian thing like fishing wasn't enough. We didn't know that what made something the Indian thing to do were the teachings that guided the process. We didn't know that all life is sacred and needs to be respected. We didn't know how to offer that respect. We didn't know this most basic of teachings because there was no one to teach us. It was only that night, after John left me alone on that hill, that I mourned the absence of teachers for two young Indian boys who only ever wanted to feel more at home on the land from which they grew.

The home I lived in was a good home. I lived with a family called Tacknyk. It's a Ukrainian name, and that family tried its hardest to make me feel like I was a part of things. For the most part, that's what I recall. But I always knew I was different. Being the only brown face in photographs was always a dead giveaway. Being teased by the kids at school because of my Ojibway name—they called me Wobbly Knees, Wagon Wheels, and the standard repertoire of Wahoo, Chief, Wagon Burner, Squaw Hopper, and Savage—was another solid indicator of my difference.

One summer it all became clear to me. It was to be my second summer with the Tacknyks, and by that time I'd grown used to calling Mrs. Tacknyk "mom" and referring to her daughter Cindy and son Bill as my brother and sister. On the surface, the Tacknyks were my "family," and I'd grown comfortable with that idea. But as spring days lengthened into early summer, the family began talking around the supper table about plans for a vacation to Riding Mountain National Park in Manitoba. As the talk grew more and more involved, I began to hear and use phrases containing the magic word "we." *We* will ride horses. *We* will go canoeing. *We* will camp out and have fires at night. I thrilled over that tiny word and began to dream about the trip. The word "we" meant that I was included, too. My excitement was almost uncontainable. As the date of our departure neared, the more excited I became. I'd never been anywhere before, and the thought of riding in the car, getting closer and closer to the fun and adventure that awaited us, was enough to keep me awake every night. Then, the day before we were to leave, I came into the kitchen after school and saw my little suitcase sitting by the door.

"Am I all packed up already?" I asked.

My foster mother looked at me from the kitchen table where she sat peeling potatoes. "Yes," she said. "We're taking you to stay with Stan and Bunny for two weeks while we're gone."

That was the first time I learned that the world can drop away from beneath your feet and that your heart can break and still keep beating.

I know that my foster-parents must have had what they thought were good reasons for leaving me behind. But no such reason can salve the betrayed heart of a five-year-old boy. That night I was driven to the other side of Kenora and dropped off with Stan and Bunny, two people I hardly knew. When the car pulled away that night, I stood in the yard waving, crying, and for the first time in my life hearing, very clearly, words in my head: "There's something wrong with you. There's something wrong. If you were lovable you'd be going along. If you were wanted you wouldn't be standing here. If you were good enough you'd be going with them." I heard those words as clearly as if they were spoken to me, and my heart was broken.

They tried to make me feel a part of things after that, but I could never forget the pain of standing in that yard as I watched the people who said they were my family drive away from me. Leaving me. Still, I was just a little boy and I clung to the hope that I would fit, that I would be one of them and I wouldn't be left alone again.

But I was.

I was adopted when I was nine years old. I'd been in the Tacknyks' home for five years—and when you're nine, five years is a lifetime in itself. No one told me what adoption meant. No one told me that it meant I was about to leave the land I loved so much or the only home I could remember. No one told me I was about to begin learning how to be someone else. All I knew was that I was going to a "new home." I didn't want a new home. I wanted to stay in the one I was in.

The last morning in the Tacknyks' home was very hard. Every minute felt painfully stretched. I was nervous and scared. I went for a walk and I cried as I stood in the bush that I loved and started to say goodbye to the rocks, the trees, the river. The taste of my tears was bitter and as I looked around at the bush that had been my playground I wanted to run. I wanted to run deeper and deeper into it, set up a camp on a point of land somewhere and live there. I wanted to go where they couldn't take me away. I wanted to go somewhere that would never change, never be disrupted, never allow me to be separated from it or the things I loved. But in the end I was just a little boy, powerless and scared, and I turned around and walked back to the Tacknyks'.

I was tossing a ball absently up and down in the yard when they arrived. When they reached out to touch me I didn't know what to do, so I just stood there staring back at them, this man and this woman who were taking me to a new home. My mother and my father. I wanted to scream at them to go away. To leave me alone and let me stay in the only place I could remember. I wanted to scream that I didn't want to go. I wanted to kick and punch and drive them away. But I was just a little boy, alone, afraid, and powerless over the big people and what they chose to do. We got in the Tacknyks' car and drove to the Kenora train station.

Remembering the event of my leaving is like watching a scene from a movie. That's how clear it is. But it is a movie in slow motion with each sound amplified and keen. My new parents and I were boarding the train. They were chattering away at me animatedly, as big people do when they're trying to soothe and give comfort. To me they were just sounds. As I looked back I saw my foster mother standing on the platform, watching me leave, waving and crying. Then, as we found our berth, I looked out the window and she was standing right outside it. As the train started to pull slowly out of the station she began walking alongside it, looking at me, reaching her hands towards me and crying, crying, crying. Her face was red with tears and grief and pain. She walked faster and faster as the train picked up speed, huge tears rolling down her face, and when she reached the end of the platform and flicked out of my sight I heard myself asking, "Why? Why are you letting them do this? Why are they taking me away? If seeing me go makes you feel so sad why don't you stop them? Why?"

But the only answer I heard were those same familiar words in my head. "Because there's something wrong with you. There's something wrong that makes you unlovable, that makes no one want you, that makes them give you away to someone else. If there wasn't something wrong with you they wouldn't let you go." I heard those words—and I believed them.

Sitting in the quiet hills above Calgary, I couldn't remember much about the train ride. What I did recall was an old black man who worked as a porter on that train. He was very kind and when my new parents explained to him that I had just been adopted and was leaving the north to go to a new home in southern Ontario, he looked at me with eyes that were wet and shiny. He nodded thoughtfully, then rubbed my shoulders and said, "Anytime you need anything, you just let me know. Okay?" Then he smiled at me, nodded at my new parents, and walked away. But every time I saw him on that trip he always had something for me—a candy, a small toy, a drink, a story. He made that trip less agonizing and as I sat in the gathering darkness years later, I realized that he had known what I was going through. Displaced people recognize displaced people, and that old black man knew exactly what I felt and did his best to make it easier for me. I was thankful for him and sad that I'd never learned his name.

The home I went to was another non-Native home. We lived in a town called Bradford in the Holland Marsh area of Ontario. That area is famous for its production of vegetables and the land is flat and treeless, with irrigation canals and ditches criss-crossing the landscape. The water in those canals and ditches is brown. I had never seen flat land before. Flat land without trees, rocks, or cliffs and no trails to follow other than the canals of brown water. I felt like I'd landed on Mars.

But as we pulled into the driveway of my "new home" my thoughts were not of the landscape but of myself. I figured that I'd better not let them know there was something wrong with me. I'd better not let them in on my secret, or I could be sent to a place even stranger than this. I decided in the back seat of that car to say whatever they wanted me to say, to do whatever they wanted me to do, go where they wanted me to go without question or fuss. That day, that moment, when I made that decision at nine years old, was when I lost myself, when I became willing to be whatever I thought the people around me needed me to be, in order that I wouldn't get sent away again, so that I wouldn't be alone. That was the day I surrendered my life to fear.

My new name was Richard Gilkinson and I recall sitting in my new room trying to figure out how I was supposed to be this new person about whom I knew no more than this. How I was supposed to be anyone at all, as afraid as I was. I was in that home for seven years and I never found the answers.

But I learned to hide quite well. I hid my feelings. I hid my hurts and pain and fear. I hid the shame I felt over being who I suddenly was—the only Indian kid around, the only adopted kid, the only one who didn't know who his parents were. I hid the anger I felt over this. I hid my resentment, and most of all I hid my fear. My hiding games were clever and no one ever found me. But then, neither did I.

The Gilkinsons tried very hard to make me feel at home. They did everything they knew how to help me feel like I was a part of things. But I had a belly full of fear. I couldn't tell them how afraid I was to walk out the door every day and be the only brown person I saw. I didn't know how to do that. I didn't know how to make sense of that. I couldn't tell them how afraid I was that there was something very wrong with me, of how I believed that if I were lovable, worthwhile, and good that my real family would have kept me. I couldn't tell them how afraid I was that when they found out how defective and unworthy I was they would send me away, too. I couldn't tell them about the deep shame I felt about not knowing anything about myself, my history, my culture, my people. I couldn't tell them how angry I was over the constant teasing, name-calling, and putdowns I endured at school. I couldn't tell them any of that because I didn't know how. All I knew then was that if I were to tell them all of the things that I was feeling then they too would send me away.

Hours had passed while I took account of this younger self. As I sat in my circle that night I made the first tobacco pouch. It was in gratitude for the sky, really. It was so clear and endless that it gave me a feeling of security. The sky could see everything. There was nothing on the face of the earth that was so small and insignificant that the sky could not see it and I was grateful for that. I was grateful because it meant that I was here, that I was a part of life, of the planet, regardless of how unimportant and lost I felt. Thinking back over my early years, I made another pouch to follow the first. The second one was for the spirit of a young boy—a lost, frightened little boy who only ever wanted to feel like he belonged somewhere. I tied that tobacco pouch for the strength that boy showed, for the courage to survive the changes, the strangeness, the displacement. As the moon rose higher over the treetops around me and the shadows grew deeper I whispered the only Ojibway word I knew at that time, the word for thank you. *"Meegwetch,"* I whispered to the universe and the spirit of that little boy. *"Meegwetch. Meegwetch, meegwetch."*

There's a photograph I recall. It's the first day of school and I am a month away from being ten. There's that curious amber light of a sunny September morning and I'm standing outside the house with my two adopted brothers on our way to the first day of school. We're in Orangeville, Ontario. At a cursory glance you would see three healthy shining faces. Brian, the oldest, tall, red hair, freckles. Bryce, the second oldest, a little plump, freckles, wavy brown hair. And me. The new one. Short, severe brush cut, thick glasses, oversized hand-me-down jacket, green slacks, oxford shoes. All of us smiling. Three brothers on their way to school—this is what you see at first glance.

But when you look closer there's more. The two white faces seem amiable, eager, accustomed to this process. But the brown one's smile is pinched, forced, ordered. Only in the eyes can you see the anxiety there. This will be my second new school in the four months since my adoption and I'm terrified all over again. I remember that morning. I walked all the way to that school as slowly as I could. I wanted to run away. I wanted to go anywhere but into that classroom where I knew twenty or more sources of agony were waiting. The photograph reveals that anxiety if you look deeply enough. I always saw it there whenever I looked at it.

The other thing you see on a more focused inspection is the sharp outline of brown on white. I was the attachment, the afterthought, a grafted limb to the family tree. That was always visible. The only negligence my adopted parents were guilty of was ignorance of the fact that I was created to be, and would always be, an Ojibway. They could dress me in all the right white clothes, send me to white schools for a white education, and try to inculcate the right white values in me at home, but I was always going to be what I was created to be: Ojibway. No amount of discipline, punishment, religion, lecturing, or preaching was ever going to make me anything other than what I was created to be. They were ignorant of that. They believed that doing their best for me, providing for me, keeping me safe, teaching me to live the way they lived would recreate me in their image. But I was never meant to be white. I was meant to be Indian and I deserved to know who I was. But I was never given that. I was never given the opportunity to learn anything about my tribe, culture, history, language, philosophy, or even a craft or skill. I was given nothing to help me learn to live as the person I was created to be.

That I was different was obvious enough to my classmates. Heading into my new school that morning I knew what to expect. The glances, the whispers, the outright finger-pointing, and the war whoops from the omnipresent class clown. Then, later, the teasing in the schoolyard, the taunts, the cruel humour of children. Later still, the fistfight with whomever was chosen to put me in my place. And later still, alone in my bed, the silent, bitter tears and the words again in my head—"See, you don't belong here. You're not good enough for them. You're unlovable, unworthy, and unwanted. If they wanted you they wouldn't treat you like this. If there weren't something wrong with you they'd like you."

That's what I always saw in that photograph. I never told anyone how I felt. I didn't know that I could. I just suffered alone until alone began to feel more natural than any other way of being.

By the time I was a teenager I was miserable. We'd moved three times. We'd lived in Bradford for three months before leaving for Orangeville. We stayed there a year, then moved to a farmhouse between Mildmay and Walkerton in Bruce County, where we stayed three years before moving finally to St. Catharines, Ontario. In every new town I went through the same agony of trying to feel like I belonged—in school, in church, in the neighbourhood. I was always the only Indian kid and I discovered very quickly that racism and ignorance has the same vocabulary no matter where you go. Name-calling, teasing, fighting, and constant putdowns were a part of my every day and I endured it all alone. I never told the Gilkinsons about any of it or how I felt in the face of it all.

I experimented. I tried leading the class in grades. I tried being the best at sports, being the funniest, the most outrageous, the most unpredictable. I tried everything I could think of to displace the fear and inadequacy I carried in my belly. Nothing worked. The more roles I played the more confused I got about who I was supposed to be, and the more confused I became the harder I tried and the more I failed. The fear of being rejected, abandoned, and isolated was stronger than anything.

By the time we arrived in St. Catharines I was thirteen. The moves left me feeling very insecure, as if my life could be disrupted at any time and I would wind up anywhere, seemingly on a whim. I was afraid to try to make friends because it always felt so terrible to have to move again and leave them behind. It felt like there was always another train station and another waving, weeping person letting them take me away again.

It was 1969. The last tumultuous vestiges of the sixties were still very prevalent in the teen culture of Dalewood Senior Elementary School where I entered Grade 8. To be cool was paramount, as I suppose it still is. Unfortunately for me there were a few things blocking my ability to achieve coolness. First, the Gilkinsons were a very frugal family. Clothes were passed down from my two adopted brothers and in an era when jeans and T-shirts were in vogue, I showed up for school in lime green dress pants, a paisley rayon shirt, and oxford shoes. My hair was still in a brush cut and the glasses I wore were what my classmates referred to as "very Jerry"—meaning the Jerry Lewis character in *The Nutty Professor*. I was ridiculed from the moment I stepped into the parking lot that first day.

Again, I was the only Indian. As the laughter followed me down the hallway to my home room I decided to do anything I could to stop the laughter. I smoked, swore, acted out in class, and lied about who I was. I chose to be the class clown and with every laugh I got I felt more like I was accepted. I began to believe that all I needed to do was get a reaction from people, that getting attention was the same as getting recognition. It wasn't. My grades fell. I went from As to Ds in one term and the resulting outcry at home was loud and painful.

But most hurtful of all was Lori. I guess all of us remember our first crush. For me it was Lori. She was a hippie, or at least as close to a hippie as her mother allowed her to be. She had long, curly brown hair that she wore under a variety of hats and she favoured the miniskirts that were popular at the time. She was beautiful—big, blue eyes, long lashes, and a smile that made her seem to radiate. When she invited me to a couple's skate at the roller rink one Saturday afternoon I almost fell over. All of the guys were after her. When we glided out onto the floor that afternoon I felt a curious mixture of being superior to every guy there and of being inferior to the beautiful and popular girl with whom I was holding hands. I became infatuated very quickly.

Lori was very "into" Indians. She had read many books about Indian people, drawn many pictures, seen many movies and television shows about them and she really wanted to "go with" a Native guy. I was the only Native person she'd ever met and she was determined to be with me. She told me all about this as I walked her home after skating that afternoon. When she asked me questions about my background and heritage I did the only thing I knew how to do: I lied.

Because I hadn't been given any exposure to my tribal identity at home, I got all my Indian information from the same place everyone else around me got theirs. I watched Westerns on television, read comic books, and went to the movies. From these I gleaned that Indians were bloodthirsty savages with a religion that was close to voodoo. We all rode horses, wore war paint, and must have been afraid of the dark because wagon trains never got attacked during the night. We were untamed, unruly, and needed the help of white people to survive. That was the extent of my cultural knowledge.

By the time I got to school on Monday the word was already out. Guys who'd never bothered talking to me before were suddenly interested in me. Girls who'd laughed and pointed at me before began looking at me out of curiosity. I felt huge. I felt like I mattered. But no one knew that I had no clue at all about my tribe, my history, language, culture, and ritual. No one knew how afraid I was that, when Lori found out that I wasn't really an Indian, she would drop me and I would be back to being "very Jerry" in no time at all. So I lied even bigger lies. I invented a language I called Ojibway—a guttural, grunting kind of talk with a lot of extraneous hand motions and gestures. I took great pains to write this new language down and commit it to memory. I gave Lori a name in that fictitious language. I told her about ceremonies I'd been to—the Sun Dance, the Rain Dance, the Ghost Dance. I told her about my grandfather the medicine man and the shamans from other tribes who had given me strong medicine so that I could survive in the city. I talked about life on a reservation and stories about life on the land.

The more I lied the more she clung to me, and the more interest she showed the more esteem I garnered at school. With the respect came a hunger for more, and the bigger and more fantastic the lies became.

I can almost laugh when I recall that performance. Almost. As I gazed upwards at the stars that night in the foothills I remembered the collapse. Lori had kept on reading about Native life while we were together and she began to detect wide variations between what I was telling her and what the books were saying and showing. I was showing her how to do a war dance and explaining the meaning of war drums to her when she'd finally had enough.

"There's no war drum. There's just a drum and it's used for many things—not just war. If you were really Indian you'd know that. But you're no Indian," I recall her saying. "You're nothing but a phoney."

She dropped me. Word spread just as quickly this time and I remember the shame and embarrassment I felt walking down the hallway to jeers and laughter. "Big Chief Full-of-Shit" was scrawled across my locker and I was alone again. All of the life I'd felt flowing through me when I was with Lori was gone and in its place was bitterness, shame, and an anger I'd never felt before. I was angry that no one, neither the Tacknyks nor the Gilkinsons, had allowed me to learn anything about who I was. They'd never allowed me to learn about my tribe, my history or culture. I knew then, in the loss of Lori, that I was no one, that all the play-acting I did was just that, that I was a non-entity because I didn't know who I was. I heard the same familiar words in my head one more time. "There's something wrong with you. If you were lovable, worthy, wanted, adequate, she'd have kept you. But you're not, she found out, and now you're alone."

Not much changed after that. I lied even more at home, school, and church, and when I was found out in those lies I was punished, banished, or rejected outright. With each reaction I became more determined to be seen, known, recognized. I skipped classes and hung out in pool halls. And I ran away from home. I ran away because even then I thought that geography was a cure. The first time I fled it was just for one night, which I spent huddled in the cab of a parked truck outside of Vineland, Ontario. It was miserable, cramped, and cold, and I actually looked forward to going back to my warm bed.

The second time I ran away, no one even knew. The Gilkinsons were away for the weekend and as soon as they were gone I took off for Toronto. I was there for two days, hanging out on the Yonge Street strip and sleeping on the couch of someone's "pad." I mooched enough to get a bus ticket back home, and was there clean and waiting when my parents arrived.

When I was fifteen I had my longest run yet. I'd been putting money in the bank from a paper route I had, and I had saved more than three hundred dollars when I took off in February. I caught a bus to Miami Beach, where I found myself in the company of three old hippies who smoked dope and hung out on the beach. I loved that. There was a laid-back feeling to that lifestyle and I allowed myself to unwind from all the stress I'd created at home. For a while I worked as a busboy in a cafeteria but was let go when I couldn't provide a U.S. Social Security Number. The money I earned was squandered on pot for my friends, movies, and lunches on the beach. I thought I would never leave. But when my new-found friends discovered I was only fifteen and a runaway, they contacted the Gilkinsons and I was flown home.

Life was horrible after that. During the weeks I'd been gone I'd got a big taste of what the world was like. I'd got a sense of the freedom that was out there, and this knowledge made me eager to escape. I couldn't tell anyone about the putdowns I endured at high school. The words were suddenly harsher, more explicitly threatening. In the early 1970s, rock and roll was king and the youth was swaying to the message of teen rebellion in the music. Everyone wanted to be considered aloof, distant, rebellious. I was far from cool and because I was different I was singled out for abuse. I so desperately wanted the abuse to stop, for the rejection to end. With every rejection from girls, every sudden silence in the hallway when I passed, every guffaw behind my back, I became more desperate for acceptance. I remember thinking that if being a rebel is what got someone recognized and appreciated, then I would be a rebel. My experience in Miami Beach had taught me a lot about rebellion.

I was relieved to find a friend and an ally right away. Doug was as much of an outcast as I was. With a face pockmarked and scarred by severe acne, he was called "Pizza Face." His mother and father were divorced and he and his three sisters lived on his mother's meagre income. His clothes were culled from thrift stores and fit as badly as mine. He was tall and gangly, with a protruding Adam's apple that jumped about in his throat when he was nervous. We shared two of the same classes and when we met one day in the smoking area—we were supposed to be in one of those classes—we looked at each other and laughed. The laughter joined us as brothers.

Soon Doug and I were going everywhere together. We'd meet on the way to school in the morning and plan our escape. As rebellious as we wanted to be, we both knew that there were certain classes that we couldn't afford to skip. Some teachers were notorious "rats" and any unexplained absence from their classes would generate a phone call to our homes. So we had to plan. Some days our designated "skips" bracketed lunch hour and we could be free for three hours or more. It wasn't long before we were regulars at the pool hall on Facer Street in the heart of Little Italy. The regulars there got to like us and began to trust us with little "missions." These errands usually involved dropping off an envelope somewhere, or picking one up and bringing it back. We always got tipped well for our time, and because we never asked any questions and were reliable the guys kept us busy. It meant we always had money for smokes, pop, and treating other rebels to pizza during those lunch hours when we had to hang around the school. I learned that acceptance could be bought for a few smokes, a small loan, and an I-don't-care attitude. I liked it.

But Doug and I were less than disciplined. It wasn't long before we were skipping whole days, then weeks. I became expert at forging my mother's signature. I would type excuse notes for myself during typing class, then scribble her signature on the bottom. By the end of the term, when report cards were due, I'd missed over a hundred classes.

For the Gilkinsons, academic failure and being absent from class were unpardonable sins. I knew I was in the deepest trouble of my life and faced, at best, the complete forfeiture of privileges. There wasn't anything I could do to change the situation, so I did what I'd learned to do. I ran away forever, carrying my problems like luggage.

It was late. Looking about I could see nothing but deep shadow. Nothing but what seemed like emptiness. I felt very alone. Every sound seemed louder, closer, more threatening. I could hear strange rustles in the grass nearby, movements in the trees and motions in the air that I had never heard before. I was scared. I had only the thin skin of the blanket between me and whatever was out there. If I had had a weapon I might have felt more secure. But I felt helpless. I began to pray. I told Creation that I was afraid, and it helped. And the longer I sat there, the more I began to realize that the living things that roam the nighttime world weren't interested in me at all. I had nothing they wanted and none of them approached very near. Unlike me, the animals had always known where they belonged, knew who they were and knew how to be themselves.

I envied them for that. I had never known any of that. My teen years were a sad mix of pain, anxiety, fear, and melancholy. I wanted so much to be included, to not feel different, that I'd ceased to care about where "in" might be. Anywhere would have done. Any group of people would have been okay. If I had been allowed to have access to my culture I might have been given teaching stories. Stories that act as guides to our selves. Stories that John told me about the animals and how they had been given the role of becoming our greatest teachers. As I sat there in that thick darkness I thought about the animals of the world and about a long story John had told me shortly after we'd met.

Before the arrival of Man, the Animal People knew each other very well and could speak with One Mind. They could communicate with each other and the Creator and there was balance and harmony upon Mother Earth.

Then, the Creator called a great meeting of the Animal People, and on the appointed day they gathered in a big circle. There had never been a need for a meeting before, and there was much talk about why the Creator would call one. No one had a clue but everyone agreed that it must be very, very important.

When they were all assembled, the Creator began to speak.

"I am sending a strange new creature to live among you," the Creator said. "This creature will not be like you in any way. In fact, it will be *unlike* you and will actually fear you."

The Animal People exchanged puzzled glances at this news. Fear was unknown amongst them.

"These strange creatures will walk on two legs, will have no hair on their bodies, will speak a language you won't understand, and will grow up believing that they must control Mother Earth."

The Animal People gasped. They knew without question that Mother Earth needed no control. Nature could always take care of itself. This would be a strange creature indeed.

"These creatures will arrive with the ability to dream. They will use this talent to create many things, things that will serve their belief in control but will also separate them from you. The further they move from you the more they will need you. The reason I called you here today was to ask you to help these strange new creatures. No one knows the world like you and they are going to need your advice and experience if they are to survive."

A deep murmur spread amongst the Animal People. This was a great request and certainly not one to be taken lightly.

"You are to be their teachers. From you they will learn how to live with Mother Earth. What I ask is very important because I also want to send these new creatures out into the world with a wonderful gift. I will give them the gift of Truth and Life. You have never needed this gift because you come out into the world knowing who and what you are. But this new creature, this Man, will not know that—and you must help him.

"I want this gift to be a search, because if I were to give it to Man openly he would take it for granted and not make use of it. So I am going to hide it. For that I need your help. I need you to tell me where to hide the gift of Truth and Life so that Man cannot find it too easily and take it for granted."

The Animal People grew excited. The Creator had never asked for their help before and they were all anxious to provide the best hiding place of all for the new creature's gift.

"I know where to hide it, my Creator," said Buffalo. "Put it on my hump and I will carry it into the middle of the Great Plains and I will bury it there."

Everyone murmured at such a great idea. "That's a strong idea, my Brother," Creator said, "but not strong enough. Because it is destined that Man will inhabit every nook and cranny of the world and he would find it too easily and take it for granted."

Then Otter stepped forward. "Give it to me, my Creator, and I will carry it to the bottom of the deepest ocean and I will hide it there."

Everyone gasped at another great idea. "Thank you, Sister," said Creator, "but Man's ability to dream will allow him to go even there and he would find it too easily and take it for granted."

"Then give it to me," said Eagle, "and I will take it in my talons and fly it to the face of the Moon and hide it there."

Surely, everyone thought, this had to be the most incredible hiding place and they were all stunned when Creator said, "No, my Brother, as great an idea as that is, it is not great enough because Man will find a way to travel there, too, and he will find it too easily and take it for granted."

This was becoming a much harder task than anyone imagined. One by one the Animal People stepped forward to suggest hiding places for the wonderful gift. One by one their ideas were put aside. Soon the Animal People began to grow discouraged. They felt like they were failing the Creator because they could not come up with a hiding place ingenious enough for the gift of Truth and Life.

Then, a tiny voice was heard from the back of the circle. "I know where to hide this gift, my Creator," said the voice.

Everyone turned to see who this speaker was. There was

a murmur of surprise. The speaker was a mole—a tiny, nearly sightless mole that rarely spoke. The Animal People moved to allow her to step forward.

"Tell us, then, Sister, where to hide the gift," said Creator.

"Where he is least likely to look," said Mole. "Put it *inside him*. Only the most insightful and the purest of heart will have the courage to look there. Put it inside him, my Creator."

And that is where the Creator placed the gift of Truth and Life. Inside every man and woman. And the Animal People became Man's greatest teacher, to fulfill their agreement with the Creator.

When Man first appeared on Mother Earth, the new creature was helpless. He had no knowledge of where he was or how to begin the journey to discover his purpose. He just sat around in the shade of a tree and watched the animals. He was fascinated by the amazing display of difference. As one by one the Animal People came by to help him, the new creature sat spellbound by the parade of animals.

Man was so enthralled that he didn't do anything. The Animal People had to bring Man food and water, or he might have perished. Man seemed content just to sit and watch. The Animal People knew that they were supposed to teach these new creatures, and they were puzzled at what seemed like laziness on the part of Man. They tried coaxing him out from under the branches of the tree he sat under. They tried sending their babies to play just beyond his reach in hopes that this might encourage Man to stand on his two feet, as was his destiny, and begin to discover the world. Nothing worked.

They sent their playful ones—Otter, Squirrel, Blue Jay—to try and get him on his feet. They sent the proud ones—Eagle, Bear, Wolverine—in hopes that he might stand in the face of such majesty. They sent the crafty ones—Weasel, Fox, Snake—in hopes they might cajole or trick the new creature up and away from the tree. Still, Man simply watched in amazement.

With One Mind the Animal People spoke to each other. This was the first crucial barrier they needed to pass to become the teachers they needed to be. But they were frustrated. Everyone came up with ideas about how to get Man on two feet and moving into the world. Every idea failed.

But one bright morning, when the sun was shining through the branches of his tree, Man saw something marvellous. From across the meadow came a floating cloud of colour. The colour danced and swooped and dipped and curled all around, inside and over itself. Man was dazzled.

Closer and closer the colour came, and as it did the more excited Man grew. He began to giggle and clap his hands in glee. He began to squirm around and reach out towards the cloud of colour. As it got nearer and nearer, Man stretched out his hands towards it until finally the cloud fluttered under the branches of the tree. It was a swarm of butterflies—brilliant, glittering, shimmering. As the butterflies danced in the air around his head, Man laughed and laughed and laughed. His hands stretched out wider and wider, farther and farther towards the cloud of butterflies. Each time, the radiant swarm moved just beyond his grasp. Finally, with playful abandon, Man stumbled to his feet and began chasing the butterflies out into the meadow. He chased them all that morning, and by the time Man realized he was hungry he had grown used to walking and running on two feet. To this day, the butterflies still dance about the heads of children to remind them of the time the cloud of dazzling wings was needed to get Man up and moving.

For the next while, Man continued to watch the Animal People. Being out from under the tree made it easier for him to follow his teachers as they made their way around the world. Man watched and learned. From the animals he learned to hunt, to gather, to store, to shelter and clean himself. He learned the rules of family, kinship, and harmony, and how to honour Mother Earth. Man began to gather the benefits of living as the Animal People taught them. Life was in balance. Life was natural.

But as was his destiny, Man began to think and dream.

It wasn't long before he was searching for his own way to do things. The simple ways of his Animal brothers and sisters seemed too easy, too relaxed. Man wanted more control. Soon he began gathering more than he needed, and greed was born. He began to take pleasure in surrounding himself with things of the world—furs, good lodges, meat— and jealousy came into being. It wasn't long before the good hunters began to look down upon the less talented ones, and judgement was created. After judgement came anger, and with anger came fear, and right on the heels of fear trotted insecurity and resentment. Burdened with these new feelings, Man began trying harder and harder to gain things, to have things, and to exploit the world around him. He began to forget the vital teachings of the Animal People and there was a great slaughter.

The Animal People were afraid. Never before had there been killing for the sake of having. Life was sacred, and when one life needed to be given to sustain another it was done respectfully and with great honour for the one that was sacrificed. But Man was killing to seem bigger and better than the others, and was beginning to try and claim the land as his own for the same reasons. When this happened the Animal People grew afraid of Man.

But they never forgot their mission. They remembered that their role was to be Man's teachers, and even though they took to hiding from him and keeping their distance, they continued to teach them. But Man mistook their distance for sneakiness and slyness and began using these against each other, too.

"What will we do?" asked Raccoon at yet another great meeting in a clearing in a forest far away from Man's eyes. "How can we teach Man when he is so eager to take us for himself?"

"He is so quick," said Crane. "As soon as we teach him another part of our way, he turns it around to suit himself. There isn't time to show him how wrong this is."

"He doesn't even try now," said Wolf. "When he hears my song he no longer tries to listen for the teaching. He only feels fear and wants to keep me away."

"How can we teach him? How can we fulfill our mission without putting ourselves in danger? How can we help him survive?" asked Beaver.

There were again many suggestions and, just as before, many rejections. No one could come up with a way of teaching that would be respectful of everyone's life. Finally, Bat spoke up.

"Man has learned by watching us," she said. "Everything he knows of the world has come from us. Every bit of his knowing has come from watching, from seeing. Well, I do not see, but I have learned to *listen* to the world in order to find my way—to feel, to experience.

"Maybe the best way to teach Man now is to let him feel his way around the world that way, too. Let him bump into things, lose things, get confused, flutter about in the dark for a while. Then he'll learn to appreciate seeing for what it is."

And that is what they did. One by one the Animal People disappeared from the world of Man. They became creatures of the dark, of the deep waters, of the highest flight, the deepest burrows, the farthest corners of the forests, the steepest peaks, and remotest valleys. They ceased to speak with One Mind in case Man, in his dreaming, might find a way to speak this way, too. They separated and Man was left alone.

Loneliness was born. Before the departure of the Animal People, Man had felt comfortable and secure in the world. Now, with his teachers gone, Man became filled with a deep blue feeling in the pit of his belly. It was an uncomfortable feeling, one he did not like and wanted far away from. But instead of turning back to his teachers for guidance, Man chose to become even more and more concerned with getting and having. He seemed to believe that getting and having was the cure for the deep blue feeling in his belly. But the more he got and the more he had, the more that feeling grew.

Soon the new creatures had divided themselves into groups. Each separate group found its own place in the world and settled there. They called these places "home." At home, Man worked hard to put great distances between himself and the deep blue feeling called loneliness. But all he achieved was to put great distances between his groups. The loneliness grew. Man told himself that the feeling came from not having enough, so he worked hard until finally he had achieved his destiny and filled every nook and cranny of the world. There were fields where forests had stood, dams in rivers and streams that once flowed strong and swift to the sea, roads where once trails had been blazed, and fences to mark where one's home ended and another began. Man had shaped his world into straight lines. He had made things predictable, controllable, secure. Still, loneliness lived in the deep pit of his belly.

The Animal People watched all of it from their hiding places. They could sense Man's desperation, and when it got to the point where they could not endure Man's suffering any longer they met in a secret valley in the mountains.

"It gets worse," said Bear. "Even though they suffer they still keep on the same path."

"Yes," agreed Turtle. "I have heard from my cousins around the world that it's the same everywhere."

"But we still need to teach them," said Rabbit. "We agreed to be their teachers at the request of Creator and they still need our help."

"That's true. That's very true," said Cougar. "But they are so stubborn. So ready to pounce on us if ever we show ourselves. Who can teach anything when all we mean to them is food or hide?"

"Maybe we should choose," said Owl.

"Choose? Choose what?" asked Porcupine.

"Not what," said Owl. "Who."

"What do you mean?" asked Buffalo.

"I mean," replied Owl, "that we should chose one group, one Family of Man, and teach them. And maybe, just maybe, that Family of Man can reach the others."

"That's a good idea," said Squirrel. "But how do we choose? And who is worthy?"

"No one. No one is worthy," said grumpy Skunk. "Everywhere it's the same. There isn't anyone living according to the teachings. No one who remembers what we taught them in the beginning. None is worthy."

"There must be someone. Somewhere," said Woodpecker.

"Where?" asked Moose.

"This is what we should do," said Owl, after much talk. "We will send out a scout. The scout will travel far and wide and if he or she can find one Family of Man that is still following the teachings, still living in the way we taught them in the beginning, then we'll come out of hiding and teach them again. But if such a family cannot be found, we will disappear forever and leave Man to his destiny. Whatever that may be."

"But who will go? Who will be this scout?" asked Honeybee.

"I will go," said a loud, distinguished voice. Everyone looked up at the branches of a nearby pine tree to see Eagle perched there. "I will be this scout. I will fly around the face of the world and try to find one Family of Man still living in the original manner. My eyes can see far, my wings are strong. I will go."

No one could think of a better scout than Eagle and so, after resting for a day, the great bird flew off on his search. The rest of the Animal People remained in the valley and bided their time with talk of the days before Man, and the legends and stories that had been born in that time. Eagle flew endlessly. From one part of the world to another he soared high above the settlements where Man had made homes and searched for people living according to the old teachings. Here and there he grew hopeful when he saw flashes of the guidance the Animal People had given Mankind, but time and again he was disappointed to see them display the new ways of disharmony.

Still, Eagle believed that there must still be Families of Man that were faithful to the teachings and so he flew and flew. He knew that if he failed to find people honouring the Earth and living good lives, he and his Animal brothers and sisters would say goodbye to Man. Man would be left without guides and teachers and he would fail to discover who he had been created to be. Eagle did not want that to happen, for despite their new separateness the Animal People loved Man and wanted very much for him to fulfill his destiny. So he searched and searched.

Back in the valley, the Animal People grew restless. Eagle had been gone for a long time and it was beginning to look as though no one would be found who lived in the original manner. But one day a great cry went up. Someone had spotted Eagle slowly flapping his way back towards them. The Animal People gathered themselves into a circle again and when Eagle finally swooped down to join them they were anxious for news. The look on Eagle's face told the story.

"I've been everywhere," said the tired bird. "I've searched from the moment I left until the moment I returned and there is no one anywhere that lives in the old manner."

A hush fell over the circle.

"Well, that's that, then," said Owl.

"It's over," said Heron.

"We've no choice," said Bear.

"Yes, yes, we do," said Eagle. Everyone looked at him, surprised. "I will go on one more circle. We owe Man that. Good teachers never stop being teachers and we owe Man the effort to look again."

"But you've been everywhere," said Badger. "Where else can you possibly look?"

"Maybe that's the problem," said Eagle. "I've been looking, searching with my eyes for what my soul wants to see. But our sister the Bat said it best when we started all of this. I'll search again, but this time I will use my *feelings* instead of my eyes. I will let my feelings guide me. That, after all, is the one true search."

So off he went. The West, the "Looks-Within Place," called to him and he flew in that direction. After a day he soared over the crest of a hill and there, alongside a stream, was a small wigwam. Closing his eyes, he breathed in very deeply as he soared over it and he felt a warm calm come over him. The more time he spent soaring over that wigwam, the more the sense of calm grew. Finally, a man, woman, and child emerged from the forest. They were carrying berries, a few fish and some herbs. When they arrived at their wigwam they made a tobacco offering and said a long prayer of gratitude for the gifts they had received that day. Eagle was impressed and settled high in a treetop to observe.

For four days he hid himself in the tree and watched this Family of Man. They prayed. They treated each other respectfully and kindly. They offered blessings back to the land. They walked gently upon the face of Mother Earth. On the fourth day, when Eagle followed them to a wigwam half a day away and saw them share their food, hides, and herbs with another family, he was filled with a tremendous joy. He raced back to the mountains to tell his brothers and sisters. There was rejoicing amongst the Animal People for the righteous family Eagle had found.

They came out of hiding. They were still willing to be the teachers Man needed in order to find his purpose on the Earth, but they were cautious. Man's readiness to take control had worried them. They had learned the truth—that knowledge and gifts too easily gained were also too easily squandered or ignored. So, just as they had once helped the Creator hide the wonderful gift of Truth and Life so that it would be a search, they would make the teachings they carried a search as well. Learning had to involve sacrifice. That is why, to this day, the Animal People venture very cautiously into the world of Man. They still come, and they always will, but it takes a careful eye to spot them, an open heart to hear the message in their call, and a spirit ready to learn the teachings they carry.

11

HUMILITY

*Beedahbun.* In Ojibway it means "first light." It refers to that moment when the edge of the visible sky becomes tinted a hard electric blue. A blue that has never been adequately represented in art or even in words, but one that anyone who has been awake at the birth of a day remembers forever. It's a blue that sears the purple darkness, burns it off and claims the sky as its own. It's a trumpet-call blue, a fanfare for the arrival of Grandfather Sun. I woke in time to see it and as I stood there shivering I felt a strange calm come over me. I didn't move. I merely stood there, locked in place, watching the coming of the light. I realized that there are colours that go far beyond the spectrum of light. Tones and tints and hues that come alive in the sky for fractions of seconds before stretching themselves thinly, elastically into another subtle, spectacular display. I saw the richest palette and as the sun began to have its way with the sky I gave thanks for the clarity that allowed me to see it.

I was cold—teeth-chattering cold—but when I began to pace around the perimeter of my circle, stamping my feet for warmth, I could see the world in all directions slowly shrugging itself into wakefulness. With the coming of the light, shadows that had been labyrinthine dungeons throughout the night skittered playfully away to the chirping of birds and the cajoling natter of chipmunks from their burrows and nests.

There had been other mornings when I had awakened in the outdoors, shivering a lot worse than I was at this moment. Mornings when I had come to wherever I'd fallen or passed out the night before—wet, cold, quaking from hangover and despair, the morning terror that drinkers endure until a splash of alcohol can chase it off. There are colours that exist in that kind of awakening, too, that have never been captured. Only they are the colours of nightmare transferred to wakefulness—sharp, cutting colours that slither and slide, creating their own unnamed perils in the shadows, which seethe with indescribable monsters and horrors. The difference between that kind of waking cold and how I felt on this morning was the difference between darkness and light. I was thankful to wake to a welcoming world.

The sun rose. The animals and birds began their days and I walked the perimeter of my circle, watching everything and feeling less alone. After an hour or so my body warmed and I sat to enjoy the breakfast of water I'd rationed out. Never had anything tasted as clean as that first sip. I made a tobacco pouch in thankfulness for water and sat there throughout the morning, working hard at keeping my mind focused on simply watching the world.

It was hard. I'd always needed to know what the next step was going to be, always had to have an out, a getaway, an alternative to anything difficult, and in that circle on the rock ledge there was no room for planning—only the world I was unused to watching. I wrestled with the desire to daydream, to fantasize as I had always done; keeping my mind within the borders of that circle was one of the hardest struggles I'd ever endured.

Then the ants came. At first it was only an adventurous one or two crawling over my blanket. They scurried about and then made their way into the grass to disappear. Soon, others came. It wasn't long before a whole army of large black ants was swarming over my blanket and around me. I wanted to swat at them, drive them away, kill them, but I remembered that I was sitting in a sacred circle and that all life within it was sacred. So I let them be. Then, I wanted to move to another part of the circle, but because it was so small there really wasn't any place to go. Finally, realizing the futility of things, I just let them have their way and do whatever it is that ants do. After an hour or so they disappeared and I never saw them again.

I thought about the ants for a long time after that. I thought about how uncomfortable they had made me, how anxious and upset, and how those feelings made me want to strike back, to conquer, to control. I made another tobacco offering. I was thankful because, in their busy scramble around me, the ants were teaching me something very important about life.

I had always struggled to stay in control, with familiar protective strategies. But the world always marched on, just as those ants had, and there was never really anything I could do about that. I could swat and destroy, or deny and ignore, but nothing would stop the march of the world. My power was small. But the power of life, of Creation, was great. Whenever I wouldn't accept change and fought against it, I was telling myself that I was bigger than life, bigger than

Creation, and really, at the top end of it, a better decision maker than the Creator himself. It came to me then that if that circle was like the world, then everything in it was equal, worth the same as everything else. The ants had just made me uncomfortable. When I wanted to either kill them or just ignore them and wish they weren't around, I was telling myself that I was worth more than they were, that my comfort was the most important thing. The ants were showing me that discomfort is a part of the world, too. Part of life. They were showing me that to appreciate being comfortable, cosy, snug, safe, I had to learn to appreciate the opposite. I had to know how it felt to be uncomfortable. Those tiny creatures were telling me that there will always be something that comes along and makes me want to do something to change it so that I can be comfortable again. But if everything is equal and worth the same as everything else, what I need to do is learn to *accept* the discomfort—change—as a part of the world and a part of life. Growing through discomfort and change and being respectful of life, chasing harmony and peace instead of conflict and irritation was, and is, at the heart of the Native way. The ants taught me that. As I sat there and looked back at my life again I realized how addicted I was to fighting change, how unaccepting I had always been of the power of the universe, the Creator's will. The evidence became clearly visible to me when I looked back at my teenage years.

When I ran away for the last time, there was only one place to run: the streets. I had a Grade 9 education, no job, no work skills, and no idea of what I was going to do. I just knew that running away from things was easier. And when I got to the street I found two things that I had been looking for all my life.

The first was acceptance. The people who lived on the street didn't care where I came from, who I was, how I felt, or what I thought. All that mattered to them was that I kept my mouth shut, did as they did, and didn't cause anyone else any trouble. If I could abide by these rules I was welcomed as just another part of the crew. I loved that feeling. After all the years of being burdened by shame and hurt, simple acceptance into a circle of people was like magic. I didn't want to be anywhere else. So I learned very quickly to choose what everyone around me was choosing and to be like they were. I grew my hair out, smoked, and behaved as much like a rebel as everyone else.

But I was never hard, never cold inside, never truly bitter at the world, society or people. I was just a scared little boy, still play-acting. I desperately wanted a home for myself, a refuge, a warm place filled with light. Every day we rebels would meet at the pavilion in Montebello Park in downtown St. Catharines. Joints and bottles would be passed around, conjuring up a lot of loud talk, play fighting and flirting with the young teenage girls who always seemed to be hanging around. Sometimes there would be a "job" planned, either a break-and-enter or robbery or even an occasional act of revenge for some perceived slight against the dignity of the "downtowners," as we were called. There was a car gang called the Night Stalkers who were our sworn enemies and a lot of energy went into planning "gags" on them. A gag was a spray painting or a tire slashing or something like that. I joined in on those talks and spoke as loudly and raucously as I could, but I always craved something more. I couldn't have told anyone what "more" was, but there was an emptiness that no amount of devil-may-care camaraderie could ease.

So I would sneak away. I would sneak off to the library and spend hours reading books. Reading always filled that emptiness for me and so I became voracious. I read history, geography, politics, architecture, astronomy, anthropology, sociology, fiction, poetry, and books on art, film, and music. There was a listening room there, and I would sit and listen to classical music and be lifted right out of that city. I filled myself with the world in those stacks and then I went back to my buddies in the park and lied.

I would tell them I'd been partying somewhere or passed out from too much dope, sex, and rock and roll. Sometimes I would visit members of the congregation of my parents' church to borrow money and I'd flash those bills around and tell my pals that I'd been off pulling a job. I told them anything that would fit the lifestyle because I couldn't tell them the truth. I couldn't tell them that passages of prose, or the quality of light captured in a photograph or painting, or the languid ache in a passage of symphonic music could set off lights in my belly and fill the emptiness there with a warmth I'd never known before. I couldn't tell them that there were ideas in the writings of great men and women that led me to a deeper world. I couldn't tell them how alive the essence of knowledge made me feel because it wasn't what being a rebel was all about.

I learned to keep my joys as private as my pain.

As I look back on that period of my life I see I was sad. I was sad because I didn't know that there was so much more that I could experience beyond the books. I thought I was stuck in Montebello Park. I believed that I deserved none of the things I was finding on the library shelves. I didn't know that the qualities of curiosity and examination were huge parts of the person I really was. I couldn't accept that because I couldn't accept myself. I needed other people's acceptance first and so I kept my refuge in the stacks a secret from everybody so that it wouldn't endanger the first outright acceptance I had ever found.

The second thing I found was alcohol.

I found drugs, too, but alcohol was what I wanted once I'd had it. Alcohol took everything away. When I had a few drinks I felt none of the burden I'd carried so long. I would be magically transformed into someone who was handsome, strong, intelligent, cool, hip, desirable, lovable, and worthy. In an instant I no longer felt about myself the way I had felt all my life and my secret was pushed way down where I couldn't feel its presence or hear the all-too-familiar words in my head. Alcohol was my magic potion. I fell head over heels, puppy-dog-eyed in love with it.

But I had created a trap. The alcohol gave me the courage to do things I wouldn't normally do—things I felt I had to do to ensure that my street buddies would continue to accept me. Things like car theft, cheque fraud, and breaking and entering. I drank to get brave enough to break the law. I was addicted to the esteem of others and I was addicted to the alcohol it took to do the things that earned me the esteem. I absolutely needed both.

Drinking became my life. When there was no money I would do a "run" or a pickup for the old winos and they would pay me with a bottle for myself. We'd sit in the bushes below an expressway where the police couldn't see us, and we'd drink and tell each other lies about our exploits until we began to pass out. Then we'd come to and do it all over again. I learned to trust the winos and they learned to trust me because I never ever "went south" with their money. Going south meant disappearing, not coming back with a bottle. Because I played by these simple rules I was welcomed into this community of despair.

Life as a wino is relentless. It's a constant to-and-fro, from liquor store to riverbank, conscious to unconscious, drunk to hung over, inebriated to sick, until it's all one endless ordeal of cheap sherry and rotgut wine. I liked them because I knew they were always going to be where I expected to find them and there was always going to be a drink waiting for me.

The winos taught me the secrets of living outdoors in a city. I learned about the haven of warm air grates in the cold, about the back doors of certain churches where a sandwich could be had, about dressing in layers so you didn't need a "tote," and how to panhandle with dignity and a certain drunken grace.

I went back and forth from the hobo jungles and crash pads to the pool halls and bars where my street brothers were. In those days, everyone had one thing they were known for. Bart was a "speed freak"—a methamphetamine user. Paradise Joe was a "head," or an LSD fiend. Chips was a "banger"—someone who did anything he could get his hands on as long as it could be shot with a needle. Everyone was known by their drug of choice and accepted, sometimes even renowned for it, based on their consumption and ability to "maintain" or stay in control. I was a drunk. For my birthday I was given a T-shirt with big white letters stencilled across the front that read, "Rick's a drunk." I wore that T-shirt proudly because for once I felt recognized, esteemed, and valued. I was a member of a club, and I saw nothing shameful in the proclamation emblazoned across my chest.

But drinking makes you careless and sloppy and it wasn't long before my attempts at crime landed me in jail. The things I did to get myself locked up were never outrageous or dangerous and the terms I served were never more than a few months. I found that gaining acceptance in lock-up was as easy as it had been on the street. The old-timers told me to "eat mutton, say nuttin." I was already good at both, so it was easy advice to follow. Being in jail never scared me. I got healthy, put on some weight, even saved a little money. When I got out I went back to the old routine—with the same result.

That's because I had no home to return to once I'd been let out. All I had was the street. I had never met anyone of substance, anyone with a predictable routine or schedule. We called such people "Square Johns," and for a street guy to be seen with a Square John was unforgivable. So I had no one to help me, no one to care about me, no one to reach out to. All I knew was the street. Concrete becomes a part of you when you get as familiar with it as I did. You become concrete. You become cold and hard. Sleeping on it ceases to be uncomfortable because you fit there. As I thought about it that night on the hill, surrounded by the whole country, I remembered how it used to feel on those nights when I would wander aimlessly, sucking on a bottle, looking for a place to rest for a bit without a hassle before moving on.

I'd look into the windows of the houses I passed. The lights seemed so warm, so inviting, so filled with life, and I imagined myself as a Square John, walking down one of those streets in the evening after a hard day's work. I would be tired, hungry. My steps would get faster the closer I got, until the moment I turned up the sidewalk of my home, when I'd slow right down. I'd slow down and look at those same windows and know in my soul that there was someone inside waiting for the sound of my footsteps. Someone who would breathe a little easier knowing I was home and safe. Someone who would rush to hug me, to welcome me, to want me near. Someone whose whole being said "love."

I craved that then, that life of which mine was the shadow. You smell when you've been drinking steadily and you can't shower regularly. Your odour makes romance impossible, except for drunken tumblings in the bushes with a woman as lonely as you are, and your lack of a telephone or address makes it hard to get a job. So the evening homecomings I imagined were light years from being possible. Still I craved them. I just didn't know how to start trying to get there.

So I'd walk through neighbourhood after neighbourhood with sadness in my chest—a heavy, thick, unmoving sadness. I'd walk until I couldn't take another step and then I would curl up in a back yard, a garage, a shed, or just beneath a tree and sleep dreamlessly and heavily. Street people don't walk with their heads down because they're ashamed or afraid. They do so because they don't want to look at what haunts them the most: the sight of contentment, happiness, sheltered lives, and warmth beyond the lighted windows. I walked with my head down a lot.

For six years I went back and forth from street to jail. Nowadays I know it was because I went back and forth to alcohol. Those six years were misery. Sober, in jail, I was in conflict with myself. I felt a great hunger within me for the opposite of what I was living. I wanted a sidewalk to walk up, a door to open, and a loved one to greet me. I wanted love, security, and peace. I wanted the magic of a good book in an armchair. But the choices I was making only ever resulted in fear, insecurity, and conflict. I didn't know how to make the things I hungered for become real in the outside world. I didn't know that my conflict was born from my spirit crying for what it needed and my mind shouting for what it wanted. I didn't know that I always chose what my mind shouted for: acceptance, belonging, the esteem of others. I didn't know that there was a way, a healing way, to bring those two parts of myself into balance. I didn't know that finding myself was an inside job. I didn't know because the choices I made always put me in a place where there was no one to teach me and make me understand.

I'd met other Native people, but only on the street, in bars, or in jail. For the most part, they were exactly like me—lost, ashamed, afraid, hurt, angry, and trying as hard as they knew how to deny it. For the most part, they were doing the same things I was doing. When they talked to me it was about the dirty deal the white man had given us. It was about anger, hatred, resentment, revenge, militancy, and getting back what was due. It was about being a warrior. It was about fighting and it was about only being around other Indians. Sadly, too, it was about drinking and being falsely proud. After that kind of introduction to who I was, I learned to react angrily over name-calling, putdowns, snubs, and other actions people sometimes take against those they don't understand. I thought it was what I was supposed to do. I added these reactions to my routine on the street and although my anger and hardness put distance between myself and others, it did nothing to bring me closer to the things I craved. It also added to my confusion.

Now I had two roles to play—the rebel and the Indian—neither of which I knew how to carry off. So I faked my way through everything—even friendship.

I had a friend back then. His name was Joe Delaney and he was a retired master sergeant from the Canadian Forces. He was a fighter, Old Joe, a tough, grizzled veteran of Korea, and he loved to tell stories of his escapades. In his youth he was a brawler, a "standup guy," a dependable friend, and an awesome enemy. His fists were as fast as his wits and he swaggered his way right into the army and upwards to sergeant's stripes. I met him through his son, who was one of the Montebello Park gang, and Old Joe took to me right away. When I'd show up at his door he'd smile and bellow, "Hey, it's the big Indian!" He liked doing that and he liked me.

For a while I went to live with Old Joe in his apartment on Cherry Street. I learned his story then and it affected my whole life. Sergeant Joe was a "slap-in-the-yap" disciplinarian who wanted his men to be as tough as he was. He was proud of his battles and as we sat in his living room many nights drinking the vodka and beer with which he surrounded himself, he regaled me with colourful stories of an army life where men were brawny, brainy, and free. The picture he painted of himself was that of an independent spirit, a fighter who would never back down from a challenge, and an unparalleled drinker.

But when the nights got long and the booze soaked through his grit and resolve, I learned the true story of Old Joe Delaney, Master Sergeant. He had been a tough young man, just as he said. He had been hard. But a girl changed all that. She came into his life and cast her gaze upon him and the Master Sergeant felt something soft and warm move inside his chest.

He fell in love. She showed him places in himself that he never knew existed, and he loved her even more for that. She took his hand and tamed him. They were married and Joe took a job as a mechanic and left the battlefields behind.

When the time was right, he retired from the army and they moved to St. Catharines, where a son was born and Joe the soldier became a husband and a father. He loved that life, and the memories shone in his face when he spoke of it, even though the booze clouded his countenance.

"I'da stayed there forever," he said. "No one ever had a better go of it than me and I prayed to whatever God there is to keep me with her always."

But a drunk driver changed all that. His wife was walking home with a bag of groceries when the drunk careened around the corner and straight into her. She was in a coma for a year. Joe went every day to be with her and he never gave up hope that his lovely bride would one day wake and return to him. And one day she did awaken. But her brain was damaged and she couldn't remember anything beyond the moment she was in. She recalled nothing of her life, of the son she had brought into the world, or the tough soldier she had tamed and loved. She couldn't speak. Joe kept on visiting her every day but eventually the blank stare from the face of the woman he loved so deeply but couldn't reach got to be too much for him.

He stopped visiting and took up drinking. Before long the arthritis born of wet mud and long marches crippled him and he was forced to leave his job. That was when I met him. It seemed like his whole life was the sofa in his living room. We'd sit there, his son and I, and he'd tell us wild stories of rebellion and bravado, shaking his fist in the air and gritting his teeth at remembered enemies, swearing, cursing, sweating, until he led himself to the memories of her and he'd cry inconsolably. Then the booze would freeze him up again and he'd pass out to the only place where memory didn't exist, where hurt couldn't enter and where old soldiers could still be brawny, brainy, and free. Oblivion, sweet and dark.

And then we stole his money.

Because we were rebels, too. We didn't care. For me, Old Joe represented free booze and handouts. I'd sit and drink his booze and listen to his tales because there was always something in it for me. He'd send me on a run for vodka and leave me the change. Every Friday the beer truck pulled up outside his door on Cherry Street and left his refrigerator full. He had his army pension and his unemployment cheques and he was careless. I always had money to try and impress the girls and whenever I needed more I'd knock on the old soldier's door. He'd always greet me with a smile and a bellow, usher me into my seat, slap a glass in my hand, and listen to whatever tale I had to tell until it was time to launch into his own.

I watched Old Joe die. He died bit by bit right in front of me. He drank and he drank and he drank until his liver couldn't handle it anymore. I watched him do that, watched him dissolve, shrink, and disappear. I emptied the bottles that he pissed in, changed his pants when he soiled himself, mopped the floor, cleaned the sofa and fed him when he was well enough to handle food. I took care of him as best I could, listened to him rant, covered him with a blanket after he'd passed out. And then I stole his money.

He died alone. I was out of town when it happened and when I heard, I dropped the phone and walked off down the road. I walked a long time. When the morning came I found a small, dark bar and had a drink for the old soldier. I had a lot of drinks that day and then I walked away, found another place, and drank some more. I hadn't been a friend. I'd been a parasite who took advantage of an old man's pain. I'd been a rebel and I had rebelled my way right past an opportunity to redeem myself in my own eyes. I let Old Joe die alone and I hated myself for that.

As I sat in my circle in the Rockies, I stared upwards at the endless sky and I cried. I wasn't crying for Old Joe; he didn't need my tears anymore. I was crying for myself, for the lost young man that I'd been. For the rebel unable to see that he was needed, that he might make a difference. I cried because my fear had made me self-centred, uncaring, oblivious to other people's pain. I cried because Old Joe had never needed me to qualify for his acceptance and friendship. It had been given as a matter of course and I hadn't seen that. I cried because if I had seen it, known it, reacted to it honestly, I might have grown up on Cherry Street. I cried for old soldiers and old rebels bearing old wounds forever.

I started another tobacco pouch. This one was for the spirit of a lost young man walking slowly through established neighbourhoods, craving the warmth and the light spilling from the windows of the houses. For his ability to survive harsh nights on the street. For rising above the heavy sadness in his chest and for moving on despite confusion, desperation, and doubt. For Old Joe Delaney and the lesson he was able to teach me so many years too late. The tears kept flowing down my face as I thought about those years and my hands trembled in the darkness as I tied that pouch together.

Then the hunger came. My belly began to groan with emptiness. When the late afternoon shadows stretched out late I could hardly think. All I could feel was the hard emptiness of my belly as it shrank in upon itself. The sun was a furnace. The humidity, with no breeze to move the sluggish air, made even the smallest breath hard to take. I stripped to my underwear and sat there with sweat coursing down my body. I wanted to swallow great gulps of water, but the canteen wasn't a large one and there were more days still to get through. So I sat there, baked and miserable.

I tried sucking on some grass. I tried sucking on small pebbles. I drank a bit of water. Nothing eased the soreness that I felt spreading from my stomach through to my entire being. It was agony. I walked around the small circle, stopping here and there to try to lose myself in the different points of view. My belly almost rattled with emptiness. Then, as John suggested, I began to tell Creation about my hunger. I talked about how good a small morsel of meat would taste right about then and about my memories of bread, eggs, milk, soup, and pecan pie. The more I thought about food the less I felt the hunger. My mind cleared and I was able to recall special meals at special times. Like the birthday party I had when I turned thirty. My friends had baked me a great chocolate cake shaped like the console of a radio station because I was working as a radio producer. They had even fashioned a long chocolate microphone. When I recalled the laughter and the friendship of that night my hunger eased even more. I went back further in my memory and recalled the great feast I had had with total strangers at a hostel on Highway 17 in northern Ontario when I was nineteen.

That summer of 1974 I decided to head out on the road again. I had hitchhiked across the country twice before and seen a lot of places. None of those places felt like where I was supposed to be and so, as all searchers do when they can't find what they're looking for, I headed right back to where I'd come from. That, of course, was St. Catharines, and I spent a long unsettled winter wishing I were somewhere, anywhere, but where I was. I wanted out so badly. Back then I thought it was the city and the life I led there that I wanted out of. But it was me. I wanted out of me because I was unhappy, unfulfilled, and empty.

I had nothing. When I worked at all it was only long enough to get a paycheque; then I'd be gone. I didn't really live anywhere. I stayed on friends' couches, slept at missions, or outdoors when it was warm enough. By then, I was already trapped in the hard rinse of alcohol. Booze still promised good times, friendship, romance, and the esteem of my partying pals, and I always chased those things. But I wanted out and I really believed that somewhere else was going to be different. I really believed that another town, another job, another party, another somewhere was going to send the magic tumblers of the universe into the proper spin and they would open the door to the world I wanted to live in. I only needed to get to the place where that could happen. So when the springtime came I began to feel the urge to go. I resisted it at first, more out of a stubborn belief that I could change things by getting a job, finding a new girl, or partying with friends, than any real desire to stay. But by summer I was eager for the road.

So, one day in July, I left. All I had was a backpack with a few clothes, two books, a bag of oranges, and five dollars. I had no idea where I was going but I knew that it was west. In those days hitchhikers were more accepted and rides were easy to get. That first day I made it all the way to Sudbury, where the great barren hills testify to the presence of the huge nickel smelters. It seemed like my journey was blessed. Day two found me outside a Husky service station in Sault Sainte Marie when evening fell. I could have walked into town and found a safe place to bed down, but I chose to try and thumb a long ride around Lake Superior with a trucker or a night traveller.

Finally, at about ten o'clock someone pulled over. He was a fishing lodge owner named Earl and he was going as far as a place called Nipigon. Nipigon is a small town at the northwestern end of Lake Superior about a hundred miles out of Thunder Bay. For hitchhikers, getting a ride around that big lake is cause for celebration because there's nothing between the Soo and Thunder Bay except for huge rolling hills and small lumber towns. Virtually no hope of a ride if you get stuck. Earl and I headed off into the night.

He talked while he drove. He told me about setting out with his father from Hespeler, Ontario, looking for land on a northern river. They were anglers. All Earl's life had seemed to have been spent on the shore of one river or another, casting for whatever fish was in season. He loved fishing. He loved rivers. And when work in the factory became too much to bear any longer, he and his father decided to pool their savings and start their own lodge. They'd found the perfect place on the shores of Lake Nipissing. Earl talked about the effort to clear a road to the site, about the two years of building, about the harshness of the northern winter, and how sometimes they wanted to give up and go back home to the farmlands of Hespeler. But their dream ran deeper than the winter snows and they finished their lodge. For twelve years it had been his life and he loved it. "Gol'," I remember him saying just before

I went to sleep, "that land just sorta cradles ya, makes ya giggle just like a baby to be wrapped up in it, makes ya wanna lie down in it forever. Guess that's why it's home."

When I woke up it was raining. Earl pulled into a service station in Nipigon and bought me a huge breakfast before dropping me at the bridge with twenty dollars and a great big handshake. He was a good man and whenever I find myself on a river fishing I wonder whether the land still cradles him, whether he still giggles to be wrapped up in it. I always hope so.

It rained and rained and rained. All of that day and on into the night the downpour continued and when I finally crawled under that bridge to sleep, it seemed like it would go on forever. It almost did. For three days I stood there with my thumb out. No one stopped. Earl's twenty ran out on the morning of the fourth day and I wondered what I was going to do. Desperation, when it becomes familiar, when it becomes a fixture in your life, only ever serves to feed itself. Nothing but booze can cleave it down to a manageable size, and that day in the rain there was no money left to get any. I thought of stepping into town to steal some money or try to stem some change on a street corner but you learn on the street to avoid putting yourself into conditions you can't control. I had no knowledge of this town, how its police responded to transients, how the people felt about strangers, or who was approachable. So I chose to suffer the rain. It seemed endless and I thought about how Noah must have felt, or the jungle peoples' amazing patience during the rainy seasons. Rain. Rain. Rain.

Then suddenly it was gone. That afternoon it stopped like a train of thought derailing. And about twenty minutes later, another hitchhiker appeared from the other direction. He was walking out to where the cars could pull over with less danger and he waved when he saw me.

"Just get here?" he asked, offering me a cigarette.

"I wish," I said. "I've been here three days."

"Three days?" he said, whistling. "In the rain? Where did you sleep? Do you have a tent?"

"No," I said. "No tent. I just crawled under the bridge."

"For three nights?"

"Yeah."

"Why didn't you just walk to the youth hostel?"

"The what?"

"The youth hostel. It's on the other side of town on the highway. Seventy-five cents, if you got it. Help with the chores if you don't. No one told you?"

I laughed. It was perfect. "No. No one told me. Maybe I should go there now."

"I would," he said. "After three nights under this bridge you deserve a good night's sleep. They have tents and bunk beds—sleeping bags, too, if you need one."

I walked two miles across town and found the hostel right where the other hitchhiker had said it would be. I'll never forget it. It was just a small house with four canvas army tents set up in the valley behind it. The man and woman that ran it, Fran and Syd—for some reason he was Francis and she was Sydney—were holdouts from the hippie days. They'd set up their hostel to help travellers like me, and it was all they really wanted to do with their lives at that point. Once they'd fed me some soup and sandwiches, they offered me the use of a steam bath. It was glorious. After three days in the wet, the heat and steam brought me back to life. I made it as hot as I could stand and when I hosed myself off with cold water I felt as alive as I ever have. When I walked down to the small valley where the tents were set up I saw that others had arrived.

There were eight of us now. At first we nodded politely to each other and went about the business of claiming our little piece of space for the night. There didn't seem to be a lot to say. By the time everyone had been able to use the steam bath, Fran and Syd came down to talk to us.

"We're glad you're all here and safe. Glad everyone got off the road okay. We really wanna say 'welcome' and ask you to make this your home. It's cool to do whatever you want here, whatever you'd do at home. We're cool with anything," Syd said.

"But we sort of have a small problem. We haven't made much money lately and we're kinda short on grub. There's ten of us tonight and we don't wanna see anyone go hungry. So we're wonderin' if everyone can throw in whatever they have and we can all make a run into town and score some food."

No one seemed to have any trouble with that. I had about fifty cents left over and I offered that. When everything was counted we had just over forty dollars and piled into Fran's old Mercury pickup for a run into town. We hit the grocery store, the bakery, and the liquor store. When we got back we had pork chops, chicken, wieners, potatoes, corn, buns, marshmallows, wine, beer, potato chips, and fruit. Everyone was laughing and talking and we fell into preparing the fire and the meal happily. Once we'd eaten and the fire had been built up we sat on upturned logs, full, satisfied, and content.

There are few things finer in this life than a good fire on a deep, dark summer night. Something about the atmosphere created by sparks spiralling crazily in all directions, the lick of blue, orange, yellow flame at the heels of the dark, the smell of fine, dry wood burning, and the game of tag performed for us by shadow and light, seems able to settle us, root us, make us comfortable again with earth, forest, wind, and the night itself. Maybe it's the primal part of us that makes it so enticing. Maybe there's still a reflection within us of nights spent huddled about a common flame, secure in the presence of family, the smell of fresh meat, and the roll of story from the old men and old women of our little bands. I like to think that. I like to think that when people around a fire disappear into their thoughts, their faces peaceful, reflecting light and memory at one time, their eyes dreamy, their hands absently poking a stick at the embers, that, in that moment, when they sigh suddenly and look deeper into the flames, they are reconnecting to that reflection, too. I like to think that because it tells me that we are all the same. Every brother and every sister from every part of the world has in common the undying reflection of fires in the night.

In itself, that summer night would have been memorable. In itself, a group of people pitching in to see that everyone was taken care of would have made for a good memory, a good lesson, and a warm story. But something wonderful happened around that fire that night.

Once we'd digested that big meal, people began making short trips to their tents. Soon there was a fiddle, a guitar, a harmonica, bongo drums, a pennywhistle, and an accordion being tuned up amidst a lot of talk and laughter. We began to sing. At first there were the usual simple campfire songs, as people relaxed with each other and got over their shyness. Then, one by one, my fellow travellers began offering more personal tunes and stories to go along with them.

The first were beautiful ballads from a Québec I had never visited but got a sense of that night. Sylvie and Luc were university students on their way to plant trees in British Columbia. They told us of hearing songs like the ones they sang on long cold winter nights around a fire in their family cabins. There was an old world charm to their songs, a waltzing sort of homesickness, that gave the feeling of rolling ocean waves and a land far behind—a land that called out to be remembered.

I heard sea shanties and Maritime ballads from Nova Scotia. They were sung by a pair of brothers from Sydney working their way back home after a year on the road. The guitar and the fiddle reeled around each other in a frenzy and the music seemed to capture the dynamic nature of the sea— lulling sometimes, calm, placid, then rolling, churning, crashing, and powerful. They were songs of a people in awe of the sea, humbled by its vastness, empowered by its gifts.

Then I heard foot-stomping jigs and reels from a Métis settlement in northern Alberta. Gabriel was a high steel worker and was headed to the skyscrapers of the United

States for work. The songs he sang that night were filled with a fire that was captivating. They were the songs of a people who celebrated the land, songs that reflected the trapline as much as they praised the furrows of farmland, songs that spoke of wagon wheels rolling across a sea of prairie grass, horses in full gallop, rifle shots, and the shadowed ghosts of the buffalo.

I listened in awe to farmers' songs. Hummable ditties of animals, harvest, and land, and small-town dreams that call youth away from pastures and plowing to the fields of opportunity somewhere down the road. Len was a farmer's son, raised in the sun-up-to-sundown world of a Saskatchewan workingman's routine. He was fed up with it and was on his way to anywhere that might hold more of everything—lights, action, adventure. His songs ached with a longing for a life of promise beyond the unbroken line of horizon.

Then came folk songs about travelling, roaming, wandering. They were songs about pretty girls in towns a million miles behind, of railway tracks, highways, dance halls, and the loneliness you feel alone at sundown. Glen was a drifter. He'd been everywhere there was to go in Canada, worked a hundred different jobs, met a thousand different people, and was on his way to meet a thousand more. The songs he sang were thick with goodbyes, solemn and final.

I listened to them all. Me, I had no songs to offer, no tales to tell of belonging, of feeling tied to a landscape or a territory, no recollections of an experience that rooted me anywhere. But I listened. Between songs we laughed, made jokes, teased and toasted each other. As song after song was sung and the fire burned longer into that perfect still, warm night we became more and more familiar. Eventually, the talk changed. Now, between songs we heard about the life of a coal miner's son in Nova Scotia, about the hardship, the ever-present feel of coal dust on clothes, food, and in the air, and about the disparity between that and the harbour with its slick wash of sea, the smell of brine and fish, and the skreel of sea birds. The nature of life with a rich Celtic vein on the gruff coast of Nova Scotia.

We heard about the Métis peoples' search for a home, about generations of children that had got used to movement, a life without roots. We heard about twelve children, six to a bed, four to a spoon, learning to snare gophers, net fish, and stone partridges to feed themselves, and the quality of joy that could be present in tough circumstances. We heard about Saskatchewan fields that ran forever and land "so flat you could watch your dog run away for four whole days before he disappeared." There were drought, grasshoppers, dust, and too many times of not having enough to make life easy. And we heard of wild meanderings through the fishing villages of British Columbia, the lumber camps of northern Québec, mining towns in the Northwest Territories, and how roaming rootless through all of it, its glory, its quiet magnificence, and its sodden ordinariness could make you hunger for more and more of it, could keep you on the road forever.

I spoke of nothing. I had no stories, no quality that made the life I'd lived up to then compelling or entertaining, but I was fixed on everything that was said that night. One by one we heard about life. Canadian life. And if there was one thing more than any other that made all those words memorable for me, it was the sameness. The geography might have been different, and the fabric of the lives a varied texture, but there was a feel to every story that reflected itself in the tale that followed it. Back then I called it sameness— now I call it *kinship*.

Eventually, the talk died down. The silence between songs and between chatter got longer and longer and the fire grew smaller. We settled for staring into the dying embers until we felt our tiredness and filed off to our bunks. I don't know about any of the others that night, but my dreams were of travels, of roads that basked in the sunshine, of fields glowing golden with grain, and a horizon that moved, inviting me beyond myself to a place and a person I had never been. They were glorious dreams.

In the morning we said our goodbyes and headed off in our own directions. I never saw any of those people again, never wrote, sent postcards, or telephoned, but I remember all of them as if it was yesterday. Something woke up in me around that fire, something that beckoned to a part of me that wouldn't be revealed for a long time, something that life needed to prepare me to find.

Night descended on my little circle on the hill, and as I considered the idea of being on the same level as everything contained within the circle I realized that the hunger I felt in my belly wasn't just for food. I had a spiritual hunger I'd never fed.

It had always been so easy to get lost in the pursuit of full cupboards. I had been so focused on getting and having that I neglected the ache I carried for the real nourishment in life. The nourishment that comes from being a part of a circle of friends, part of a community, part of a people, and the potent vitamins of love, acceptance, loyalty, trust, and honesty that come from sitting around a common fire.

I had never really fed myself. The more I thought about it the more I came to realize that food is a great coming together. It has the ability to pull everyone we love around a table, around a fire or around a room, and as much as we feed our bodies at these moments, we feed our souls, our spirits, our beings as well. Even solitary meals could be like that. When we give thanks to Creation for its generous spirit, and ask for the food for our bodies to nourish our spirit, and for the strength of that spirit to be available to help someone else, we have fed an appetite no less aching than hunger.

I began to cry again. I couldn't help but wonder why it seemed like tears were the price of admission to this ceremony. It bothered me. I didn't like crying, but I cried through the baying of coyotes, the flicker of fireflies, and the dive-bombing of mosquitos. It wasn't a weeping born of loss, nor was it a release of guilt or sorrow. Instead, the tears I was shedding were for the loneliness and isolation of a young man by the side of a highway in the warm rain of summer. A young man bent on being anywhere but wherever he found himself. A young Native man, scant yards away from the land that could define and sustain him if only he reached out to it, if he'd only known how. I cried for the feelings of shame, frustration, fear, anger, and melancholy that that young man carried, the feelings I felt rekindled within me. I cried because travellers eventually get weary of the road. Nomads, seekers, and escapists tire of the constant motion and crave stillness—a settling down—but after so many miles they forget how to reach for it and their hands remain as empty as their hearts. I tried to imagine what I would tell that young man if I could—what messages of hope I might offer, what alternatives were possible, what was coming for him around the next bend in that road. But we are not graced with that ability and as I sat there moving into the depths of that second night I learned that it's possible to hold the people we have been in our lives close to our chests and offer comfort. I held that young man a long, long time that night and I told him a story about a great coming-together.

In the Long Ago Time there was great trouble among the People. The animals had not come and the People grew hungry. With their hunger came anger, jealousy, and bitterness. Those who were fortunate enough to snare a few rabbits or net some fish were reluctant to feed their neighbours and there was deep resentment all around.

This time of scarcity was hardest on the men. Ojibway men are proud hunters and fishers and there is much honour in being able to provide for one's family and village. Watching their families suffer brought many heavy feelings to the hearts of the men. It wasn't long before shouts, arguments, challenges, and fights broke out amongst them. Even friendships of many years were threatened by the anxious feelings in their hearts, and the villages were tense and the women and children feared the anger they could feel in the men.

As time went by and the shortage of food grew more and more severe, things grew more desperate. What little game was available came to be seen as something to be hoarded rather than something to be shared. Some men stole food from other villages, others destroyed the traps and snares of their fellow hunters. Gill nets were slashed and no one was praying for the animals or offering tobacco gifts to Creation for a good hunt. With the loss of their spiritual way of hunting, greed became the biggest force amongst the men.

The greed spurred them to fighting. Soon village was setting out against village over some injustice imagined or genuine. Blood was spilled and it seemed that the great circle of the People would become torn apart from within.

One night, as a council of men was meeting to plan an attack on a distant village, a strange thing happened. Beyond the trees they heard a sound. It was a sound unlike any they had ever heard before but it was also very familiar. It grew louder and seemed to echo all around them until, at its loudest, the sound filled the entire night. The men were frightened. It sounded to them as if something very ancient and strong was coming their way.

Then a light was seen. A dim yellow light that shone against the tops of the trees. The men could see it moving from treetop to treetop as the sound grew louder and closer. And closer and closer. Despite themselves they shuffled together in fear. The light kept coming and the sound continued. Some of the men wanted to run but they were held in place by their pride. The light grew brighter.

Finally, they could see something walking within the light as it began to emerge from the forest. It was a woman. A very beautiful young woman in a dress of the purest white buckskin. Around her neck was an amulet of shells that hung in concentric rings so that it looked like the breast plate of a warrior. Braided into her long black hair were two eagle feathers, and on her feet she wore ankle-high moccasins beaded in a floral design of purple and orange. Purple is the colour of spirituality and orange the colour of old wisdom, old teachings, so the men knew they were seeing a holy woman. Her dress was fitted with beaded designs in the same purple and orange. As she moved closer, the men could see that her eyes were closed and her face was raised to the night sky above with a look of deep reverence and peace.

In her hands she held a strange object. It was round and looked to be made of wood. Dried skin was stretched taut over it. The woman was beating on it with a stick—this was where the deep echoing sound was coming from. She walked slowly into the middle of the circle of men and continued to beat on the object. When she had reached the exact middle of the circle she stopped.

No one drew a breath. Stillness. Quiet. Then, very deliberately, the beautiful young woman began beating on the skin of the object again.

*Boom-boom-boom, boom-boom-boom, boom-boom-boom,* was the sound it made. The men looked wide-eyed at each other in fear and wonder. Then, the woman began to sing.

"Hey, yah-hey, yah," she sang in time with her beating. "Hey, yah-hey, yah."

Her voice was pure and the men were hushed by the power of this strange and wonderful song. She went on. She faced each of the Four Directions and sang her song through. When she finished, facing the North, she gave four very heavy beats on the skin of this strange object, raised it to the sky like a blessing, lowered it slowly toward the earth, held it there a moment, then opened her eyes and looked at the nervous circle of men.

Her eyes were like the darkest crystals. They shone and glimmered with a light that enchanted all of the men. It was a light of kindness, of compassion. It was a light of Love and of Spirit. No one said a word.

The woman began walking slowly around the circle, looking at each man in turn. When she had made the complete journey around the circle she stopped and held the object out in her hands.

"I have come from the Land of the Spirits," she said in a voice that was both humble and strong. "We have been watching you and we have been distressed at what we have seen. You have allowed this time of scarcity to take you away from the Teachings. Instead of sharing and living in harmony with each other, you steal and fight and plot against each other. Instead of living in gratitude for what you have, you live in anger for what you do not have. Instead of seeking to live in balance you look for advantage, for gain. We have felt the spill of your brothers' blood upon the land and we have heard the cry of your mothers, wives, sons, and daughters over the hatred that grows among you.

"We have decided to give you a gift to remind you of the way in which you are supposed to live your lives. A gift that will remind you that you are connected to everything and that you have a responsibility to look after and care for all things. This gift is called Drum. It is made from the trunk of a tree and the skin of a moose to remind you of reverence and respect for all living things. It is round like the wombs of the mothers that gave you life and like the Great Circle of Life that feeds and sustains you. The song it sings is the song you heard in darkness as you lay in your mother's womb. The heartbeat.

"When you were being born that sound comforted you. In that warm darkness of your mother's belly, that sound told you that all was well, that you need not fear. Now, whenever you play this Drum you will be comforted again because you hear the heartbeat of your mother and of your Earth Mother. You will want to join your heartbeat to the heartbeat of Creation coming from this drum.

"I will teach you how to do that."

And the woman showed the Drum to the men. When they were assembled around it in a circle she taught them a song. Their voices raised together to fill the night. They were shy at first. The power they could feel coming from the Drum and the power it gave their voices as they sang with it filled them with reverence and awe. Slowly they became more confident. Then they were singing, loudly, passionately, and well. Within them they could feel their spirits joined with the spirit of Creation, their heartbeats joined with the heartbeat of Drum, of the universe, of Mother Earth, and their anger, hatred, jealousy, and bitterness faded off into the deep blue of the night.

When they had finished, the woman showed them how to care for Drum. She taught them how to cleanse it in the smoke of the sacred medicines of tobacco, sweet grass, sage, and cedar. She taught them how to warm it in the glow of their fires, to stretch its skin taut and firm so its voice would ring. Then she taught them to pray with it and to ask for their voices to be joined together in harmony with Drum. Several men were chosen to be makers of the Drum and she taught them the rituals and prayers involved in the gathering of the elements of Drum. When she had finished she prepared to leave them.

"Always remember," she told them, "that Drum comes from the spirit of Woman. It is round like her womb. It is life-giving like her spirit. It is healing like her love, forgiveness, and nurturing. Honour your women. Protect them, provide for them, learn to walk in balance with them. Drum will always remind you of those duties."

Then she turned and began to walk away. The men watched her as she walked. As she got further and further from the fire her steps got slower, shorter, less firm. When she reached the edge of the forest again she turned to face them. They gasped. In the place of the beautiful young woman they had spoken with was a Grandmother. The Old One smiled at them and they saw the same eyes of gleaming dark crystal. She was beautiful. In her smile the men felt blessed, and as the Old One disappeared back to the Land of the Spirits they raised their voices together in an Honour Song to give thanks for this strange and wonderful new gift.

# III

## INTROSPECTION

I woke in the rain. Sometime around dawn the clouds had moved in and the rain started pouring down in sheets. My little circle quickly became muddy. My blanket was sopping wet. My hair hung over my eyes, plastered to my face by torrents of water. I shivered. There were trees a footstep away from the edge of the circle and I wanted to step over and sit beneath their branches for shelter. I craved shelter as much as I had hungered for food the night before. It rained and rained and rained. I felt miserable. I pitied myself. I bemoaned my decision to come here and the difficulty in learning this way, its senselessness, its hardship. The trees and the bright dry spot beneath them looked like a palace to me. I agonized over whether I should step out of the circle and into the trees. I wanted to stay where I was and learn whatever I was going to learn about myself, about the Native way, about the world, and about my right place within it. But I was cold, shivering, miserable, alone, and afraid. Once again, I did as John suggested and admitted my feelings to Creation. I talked about my agony and I felt the rain grow warmer. As I stomped around I vented my frustration and I began to feel more at ease. Then I realized that the rain felt good. For two days I had sat in the sun, wind, and dust, sweating out all kinds of things my body had absorbed. The rain was washing all of that away. The more I focused on that fact, the less I wanted to abandon my circle. Soon I was holding my face up to the rain and feeling the cool water splash against my eyelids. It was refreshing. Not just because it soothed the dust and dryness of things, but because it seemed to wash away the purple stain I felt inside, the one that revisiting myself and my life had created.

I thought about the reasons John might have had for bringing me to this point in his teachings. I needed release. I needed to be free from the stranglehold in which my past held me. I needed to cut the ropes of shame, guilt, and fear, to see my life for what it had been and walk forward to a better way. Those were the reasons he'd decided to bring me here. And as much as I understood, though, I still felt the cold nuzzle of fear in my belly. The habits that nearly killed me were still my crutch—and I could not imagine life without them. I didn't know how I was going to acquire, or even if I had the ability to acquire, new skills, new tools, new ways of being.

The rain slacked off to a drizzle, then to a light mist. Finally it stopped completely. I was relieved. I lay my blanket flat on the ledge to dry. It was cool but I removed my shirt, too, and did some jumping jacks to get my blood flowing and warm myself. When I felt the goose pimples disappear from my arms I sat down again and looked outward over the trees. My eyes came to rest on something so commonplace, so ordinary, that it had escaped my attention all the times I had visited that ledge.

It was a tree, no more than a twig really, sticking out from a small cleft in the ledge. It was sparse and dry and twisted. It looked as though it should be dead, as if its roots had no soil to grip that rock. But it lived. There was a tiny clump of foliage near its tip and the fresh rain glistened on it. I don't know how I could have missed it all along but right then I was riveted to it. Strange as it seemed to me, I felt as though that little tree was trying to tell me something. So I sat and watched it, studied it, and waited for its message.

I began to think of how hard I had sought a footing in my life. I thought about the struggle. Then, I remembered a time when the battle had grown too hard and I had given up, surrendered, capitulated, and become willing to allow the world to toss me where it would.

I was twenty-three years old. That summer I had taken off again and headed into the west. When I arrived in Regina, Saskatchewan, I stopped to look around for work. The only place I could afford to stay was the Salvation Army, and I hated it there. But I needed to earn money to keep on travelling so I gritted my teeth and held on. But I was never too good at holding on and eventually I went to the bars in search of those things I knew how to deal with. And I found them. It wasn't long before I was in the company of a group of young Native people who were just like me. They were drinkers, hardcore and remorseless, and they were lost, dispossessed, and angry.

They welcomed me as a brother because of the colour of my skin, and if I didn't know anything about my language, culture, or history it didn't seem to matter to them. All that mattered was that I was another "skin"—short for redskin—and that I would do as they did. We drank. Lots. There were fights, brutal ones sometimes, that even the women joined in. Fights with baseball bats and knives, broken beer bottles, and even a rifle once. But there was camaraderie, laughter, and a caring that reminded me of the winos I'd hung with years earlier. They helped each other when they were sick with the drink, and nothing was too much to ask if you needed help. I wanted to be a big part of that so I listened and learned.

Many of the young men in our group had grown up under the influence of militant Native groups like the American Indian Movement. They wore their hair long, in braids or long ponytails, and they weren't ashamed to wear colourful patches bearing one message of solidarity or another. They were pro-Indian and anti-white. There was no middle ground or room for negotiation in that. From them I learned about the genocidal policies of governments in Canada and the U.S. I heard for the first time the story of the residential schools and how generations of our people had been abducted from their homes and sent to learn the white man's way. I heard how language had been lost, ceremonies outlawed, how Indians had needed a pass from the Indian Agent in order to leave the reserve, how it had been illegal for them to meet in groups, that we hadn't even been allowed to vote until 1960, and that recent government policy had been directed at making Indians a part of the mainstream, abolishing the Indian Act and the reserves—the heinous "White Paper on Indian Policy."

I heard all of that and more. It wasn't long before I had a red headband, the colour of AIM, and was reciting the rhetoric I had adopted from my new "brothers in the struggle." I became racist in my thinking and it was easy to blame the white man and society for my ordeals. In fact, it made more sense than anything I'd thought of or heard before. It had never been me that had caused my troubles—it had been the bigoted hand of the white man that yanked me from my family, tossed me into a foster home, adopted me, tried to make me white, and then threw me into prison when I couldn't or wouldn't assume his colour or his thinking. My life finally made sense to me and I had a purpose.

Unfortunately, I continued to drown that sense of purpose in alcohol. Trying to fit in with this new group meant that I believed I needed to prove myself. I drank even more to screw up the courage to be outrageous. Somehow, during a blackout, I managed to get hold of a credit card. When I came to, there was a large group of us in a motel room somewhere outside Regina and the party was in full swing. It scared me to think that I'd done something I couldn't remember and I grew fearful of being arrested. The next morning I left. I used the card to get a plane ticket and fly back to Ontario where I used it to keep on drinking, stay in good hotels, buy clothes, and keep on drinking. Finally, I was arrested, charged with fraud, and jailed for ten months.

Over the six months I spent in custody I continued to read pro-Indian material. I devoured *Bury My Heart at Wounded Knee, God Is Red,* and *The Indian Manifesto.* The only friends I allowed myself to make in jail were other Native men with whom I shared my beliefs in the wrongs of the white man. I came to the belief during that stretch of jail time that being an Indian meant being a warrior, fighting against the power structure, fighting to bring that power down and restore the people to their rightful place as owners of this land. My hair grew longer as my resolve deepened. This, I remember thinking, is what I had been looking for all my life.

I decided to live without the few privileges jail offered. The white guards and the white warden wouldn't get me to buy into their cycle of dependency. I went without canteen supplies and saved the incentive allowances we were allowed at that time. When I was released after six and a half months I had a few hundred dollars in my account, and my plan was to head back west where I imagined the heart of the Indian rebellion was centred.

But I'd made a friend while I was inside and he had talked endlessly about the hot rod he was fixing up in his mother's garage in Toronto. He'd shown me pictures, from the day he'd bought it at a junkyard, right through the restoration process to the point where it was rebuilt, fitted with a new engine, and primed for the paint job he wanted to do once he was out. So I went to visit him and see this car before I caught my bus to western Canada.

We had a great visit. It was good to see a "brother" on the street. I met his family, we drank some beers, and we tinkered with his car. Early that evening I left to catch my bus. As I was leaving he tossed me a black denim jacket. The back was emblazoned with a bright red fist clutching an eagle feather. "Red Power" was written boldly beneath it.

"You'll need this," he said, and he smiled.

"Thanks," I replied. "It's great. You sure?"

"Oh, yeah," he said. "Besides, it looks better on you than on me."

We hugged and I left him. Walking down the street I felt filled with pride. The emblem and the words on my back gave me strength. I believed that I walked taller and prouder just wearing it. As I passed store windows I looked at my reflection: a tall, lean, long-haired Native man with a headband and a Red Power jacket looked back at me. For the first time in my life I felt fully dressed.

I was lost in the thoughts of what I would do once I got back to Regina and I didn't notice the police cruiser until it was blocking my path across a laneway. The two officers got out and stood in front of me.

"Where you headin', Chief?" the one asked.

"Bus station," I said.

"Oh, yeah?" his partner asked. "Where'd you come from?"

"I came from Burtch Correctional Centre," I said. "I just got out this morning. I'm heading home."

"That right? Well, you won't mind if we search you then, an upstanding citizen like yourself."

I had nothing to hide and I'd been honest, so despite the anger I could feel boiling in my chest I leaned against the wall and allowed them to frisk me. I figured I'd be on my way in a few minutes.

"Well, well, what do we have here?" I heard and I was twisted around to face the two of them. In his hands one of the officers had the small screwdriver and two thin wrenches I'd been using in my friend's garage and forgotten about.

"Tools," I said. "I was working on a friend's car and I forgot that I had them. If you want we can go back and ask him."

"That where you got the three hundred, too?" the first officer asked.

"That's what I saved during my bit," I said. "You could check that, too, I guess."

I was put in the back of the cruiser while they ran my identification on the computer. It came up clean, as I knew it would. No wants or warrants. But it also showed my record.

"Seems you've been a pretty busy boy. Break and enters, too. You know this area's been pretty bad for B&E's lately and here you are with burglary tools in your pocket and a bunch of money," the second officer said, turning back in his seat and fixing me with a hard glare.

"I told you. I was helping a friend fix a car and that money's what I earned in Burtch."

"You been drinking, too, Chief. So I think we're going to take you in for possession of burglary tools. What do you think of that?"

I was stunned. I couldn't believe what I was hearing when all that was needed was for them to drive me back to my buddy's and things could get straightened out. Then I remembered all the things I'd read and learned over the past year. That was my mistake.

"I think you're both a couple of pigs and if I was Joe White Guy walking down this street you wouldn't even have bothered. But you see an Indian, you gotta pull a move. Pigs," I said. "Couple of fuckin' pigs."

Twelve hours after I'd been released I was back in lock-up. When they closed the door to my cell that night I laughed. It was all so ridiculous that anyone with an ounce of comprehension would see the situation for the charade that it was. My anger boiled over and by morning I'd decided that I would make a mockery of the whole thing. I'd plead guilty and once the facts were revealed, the judge and everyone in that courtroom would see how ridiculous it was. I didn't need a lawyer. To me, at that instant, a lawyer was just going to be one more white man I didn't need and this whole thing was silly anyway.

I was sentenced to six months.

For a whole week I spoke to no one. I paced the cell block and I thought. I thought about how I'd been judged on the way I looked, on what I represented. I thought about my place in the world—a place and a world that seemed beyond my control, defined and arranged by an order of others, comprised of anyone who had ever done me harm, that I could think of only as *they*. I had been tossed away as something unimportant, something inconsequential that *their* system wanted out of the way. I was an Indian and because I chose to express my identity through long hair and clothing *they* decided I needed to learn my place. My place apparently was not on the streets of *their* city. I was a threat to *their* peace of mind. The anger over the injustice of what had happened to me felt hot and rancid in my throat. I burned with it.

In the end I decided that I wasn't going to play nice any longer. If *they* were responsible for the struggles of my life, if *they* were to blame for everything I'd gone through, for my sense of being lost, for not knowing about myself or my culture and heritage, then *they* were going to pay. If *they* could say that I was a criminal and put me where *they* figured I belonged, then I would prove that *they* were right. I would rebel, and hard. I would cease to care. I would get out and get all that I could for myself without regard for anyone else.

I needed a symbol of my rebellion. Until then I had never had a tattoo, although "tatties" were considered strong symbols of a rebel heart. My next-door neighbour was a tattoo artist, and he'd rigged up a homemade needle that he'd used to tattoo other men. It cost me a couple bales of tobacco, but one night he drew a marijuana leaf on my right forearm. It hurt. The needle was made out of a thread-wrapped pencil that held a darning needle. The needle was dipped in ink and then jabbed continuously in the desired emblem. It took about an hour, and with each jab I clenched my teeth and allowed my anger to numb the pain. Then it was over. I was going to war. I would be a warrior and screw anyone else, and especially screw *them*. They could do what they wanted with me. As long as I could know that I was fighting back, tossing it all in their faces, showing them that they had created me, that I was their invention and their punishment.

The sun came out. It flashed on that little tree in the rock like a spotlight and I snapped back to the ledge. That little tree was rebelling, too. It was refusing to die. It was choosing life despite its desperate circumstances. No matter how difficult the climb, that little tree was reaching for the sky, reaching for all that it could be, for its truest expression of itself. I admired that little tree. I had never had that kind of courage. And as I looked back at those days of my imprisonment I saw that I had been willing to cling to any cleft in any rock at any time. I'd been willing to become a militant warrior. I'd been willing to be a rebel, a career criminal, and a revolving-door inmate as long as I didn't have to face myself as I really was. And the truth was that I had been a scared little boy all along, terrified that someone would uncover my secret, know me as flawed, unworthy, and send me off alone again. Because

I had been that little boy, the only cleft I clung to that lasted through everything was the cold, hard rock of alcoholism.

I didn't become a warrior criminal. I didn't become an activist. I didn't become a passionate upholder of Native rights. I was released and became what I'd always been, a drunk. My prison anger didn't save me. It didn't transform me. Neither did the rhetoric of rebellion or militancy. They just made it easier to pop another top and drown the confusion, pain, doubt, and fear that drove everything, even the anger.

I was grateful for that little tree and I made another tobacco pouch for its teachings. It was showing me that there is courage in merely hanging on. It was showing me that nature—life—will always find a way to its truest expression of itself. It was showing me that growth happens invisibly, where we least expect it, in forms that sometimes surprise us.

I thought about the rain I'd endured. It had shown me that the gifts of the world—the wind, rain, snow, heat, humidity—all work to a purpose. Beforehand, I could only see the discomfort they caused me. My discomfort led to being critical, complaining about the lack of comfort in my life. I saw now that it was always going to be either too hot, too cold, too wet, too dry, too dark, too bright, or not enough of any of them. The rain, like the ants before them, was telling me that I am a part of Creation whether I like what's happening or not. My purpose, like that of all Creation, is to continue. Creation is intent on continuing towards its best possible fulfillment of itself—because that is the reason for life. I saw then, in that tree in the rock and the rain, that I needed to continue on towards the best possible fulfillment of *me*—the best I can possibly be—despite what was going on around me. The rain taught me that and I was thankful.

That third night I was past the point where hunger was painful. I didn't need much water, either—wetting my lips was enough. I saw the sun set. Everything around me was pulled into sharper focus and I felt like I was seeing things for the very first time. As the colours exploded over the top of the mountains, they faded into softer, then darker shades. I had conquered hunger, thirst, rain, insects, discomfort, fear, and the desire to quit. I had beaten them by accepting that I felt them and continuing on despite them. I had shown courage. As the light faded and the world eased into sleep I came to experience solitude in a way I never had before. Other times solitude was a weight that pushed me down and down into depression, self-pity, fear, and a sense that I would never be enough—enough of a man, enough of a person, friend, worker, lover, or smart enough, funny enough, handsome enough, strong enough, talented enough, rich enough—for people to really want to be with me. I feared being alone more than I feared anything else. And the reason I feared being alone was that I had never felt right with myself—didn't like myself, appreciate myself, or even love myself enough to be comfortable in my own company. Up to that point I believed that if I didn't like being with me, no one else would either.

There was no longer a need in me to be anywhere else, to surround myself with strangers so I wouldn't feel alone, or to want to run to some other place so that I could lose myself in the running. Instead, I belonged on that hill. I thought about all the places I had travelled to, all the people I had known, all the things that I had tried to feel like I was in the right place. And I made a tobacco pouch for all of them because they had all led me to that hill. I looked up at the universe and found all my favourite stars. I listened for the sound of the owls as they flapped their heavy wings through the night in search of game. I waited for the coyotes on nearby hills to begin their shrill yipping at the moon. The night was inhabited by many beings, and I was one of them. And that was when it hit me. I *belonged*. Just as I was, I belonged. And the truth was, despite the feelings I had carried around about myself all my life, despite the beliefs that I wasn't enough, I had belonged all along.

When I was twenty-four, jail ceased to be a place where I lived regularly. Instead I found work in the Native community as a reporter on a small Native newspaper. It was there that I began to find the parts of myself that had been missing all my life. I found elders who knew of the old ways. I found traditional people who knew and followed the teachings. I found young people like me who were making the journey back to themselves. I was not alone in being alone. It had not occurred to me that I was not the only one ever adopted, the only one who didn't speak the language of his birthright, the only one who knew nothing of his tribal self, the only one who felt ashamed, unworthy, and afraid. But just knowing this wasn't the whole answer. It still didn't make the hurt go away.

I went to ceremonies and gatherings where the ancient teachings were discussed and passed on. I went to powwows, feasts, exhibitions, festivals, and celebrations where our cultural way was shown to thousands. I was given the opportunity to learn about myself, my history, culture, language, and belief system. For once, I put myself in a place where there was someone to teach me and I came to understand.

But understanding is not healing.

I had never been to a Sweat Lodge. It was something I had heard about and found myself wondering about at times, but I had never participated. I was afraid. Afraid that this ceremony would expose me. But one day someone showed me a glow in the darkness. The glow was the traditional teachings of our people. The more I engaged with the Native community, the more I began to see people who were trying to live as close to traditional teaching as possible. I watched them closely. In their actions I saw kindness, generosity, warmth. I listened when they spoke and in their words I heard understanding, empathy, compassion, and love. They showed me, by the power of their life as they lived it, that traditional ways were powerful ways. And I was attracted to the glow of their lives. When you've lived your whole life in darkness a glow, a light, is something you can't resist.

I met some of those people after a while. We became friends. They talked to me about our way. They showed me by their example how someone can live well and happily by walking our path. Bit by bit I began to understand. Then I began to put that understanding into practice in *my* living. Not in a huge way, because I wasn't ready or strong enough yet, but I made some small progress. After a time I started to feel connected, rooted, tied to the tree of tradition, and I knew that it was time to start my journey to the light.

They told me that choosing to stay in the dark, as I had up until then, was not wrong. In our way, we can choose anything. In fact, our whole path is a pathway of choices. When we choose we create, they said, and our purpose here is to create ourselves, to *experience* ourselves, our souls. Choice is the power the Creator gave us to be able to do that.

They told me about the Sweat Lodge. They told me how they had made the same journey I was on and that the Sweat Lodge ceremony had helped them get past the pride and fear that held them back. That was good news to me— that people I admired had battled the same pride and fear. I wasn't that different after all. So I agreed to learn this way.

Under the guidance of two men, Cliff and Walter, I began to try to open my mind and allow a teaching to enter my life. It wasn't easy, because stubbornness is quite often the bulwark of fear and it took a lot of convincing to get me to the point where I could begin to see how much this ceremony offered me. Cliff was a Sioux and Walter was a Plains Cree man. Despite their different tribal backgrounds both men respected the Sweat Lodge ceremony for its ability to help people heal themselves. For them it was the basis of a tribal life and they were eager to help me to learn.

The first thing they taught me was that the Sweat Lodge ceremony is about humility. The word *humility* comes from the same root as "humus" or "earth" and the way Cliff and Walter saw it, humility means to be like the Earth. The Earth is very humble. Humility allows others to pass, to grow, to reach for Father Sky from the same arms of Mother Earth. Humility allows everything to be as it was created to be. So the Sweat Lodge begins with the Earth.

I was told that the beginning of the ceremony required me to go out and walk upon the land. These first steps through the bush were the beginning of a long journey. As I walked I was to try to pray and meditate upon the ceremony I was about to perform and ask for the humility to see it through to the end. While I was performing this "Spirit Walk" I was to look for rocks to be used in the ceremony. These rocks are called Grandfathers, because they are ancient and have been upon the Earth a long time. After these countless lifetimes spent upon the Earth the Grandfathers are wise and have many teachings that they will reveal in the ceremony. When I came upon a rock that seemed right, one that caught my attention, I was to offer a pinch of tobacco, say a prayer of thanks and a petition for strength, and gently carry it to the site chosen for the Sweat Lodge. For my first Sweat Lodge I made forty journeys for Grandfathers. Each trip is like a day in your life. In the early morning I went to and fro, back and forth, for hours.

As I walked I fought a lot of battles with myself. And all the walking made me feel that the Sweat Lodge was senseless. I wanted an instant fix, as though finding a spiritual way of life was like some drive-thru where you could make an order, pay for it, and continue on your way. I wanted to be able to order a double humility burger and get going. But I began to see that this walk was a lot like life itself. As long as I focused on the repetition life became stale. I lost my creativity—the spark of life—and my focus dulled. But like the process of that walk, if I concentrate on picking up something eternal, ancient and healing on each day of my Earth Walk, something that could teach me how to become who I was created to be, then my walk is en-*light*-ening. That's why the Sweat Lodge ceremony begins with a walk upon the Earth.

Cliff and Walter and I talked about this idea when I'd collected all forty stones.

"Everyone wants to live a Shake 'n' Bake life," Walter said. "Nobody wants to have to sacrifice anything to learn. But sacrifice is always the price of admission to another level."

"You're giving up your day to do this," Cliff said. "That's a sacrifice. You're letting go of your pride, you're willing to let someone teach you, you're admitting you don't know. Those are all sacrifices. Without them, without making them, you wouldn't have reached this point."

"Now that the Spirit Walk is completed we're going to build a fire. We'll lay logs down like a bed and pile the Grandfathers on top of them. Then around and over the Grandfathers you will sprinkle tobacco and pray in your own way to ask for the help of those Grandfathers. Then we'll place more wood over all of them."

We set to work. They were very methodical, very gentle and easy in their movements, and I took special care to be as attentive as they were. We worked in a silence that was scary to me. It gave the whole process a liturgical quality that spooked me, as though I were making a commitment I might not be able to keep. I felt a thin coil of fear wrap itself around my belly. But whenever our eyes met, Cliff or Walter would grin at me and it helped ease the anxiety I felt.

Once we'd built the wood and stones up into a high pile I was sent to gather some dry birch bark from the bush while they sat and smoked. When I returned with an armful they were waiting, laughing, and joking casually. Under Walter's direction I placed hunks of bark randomly amongst the stones and wood.

"Rock and fire were the first elements the Creator used

when he created this world and so they are the first part of the ritual," he said.

When the fire got going we picked up a shovel and Cliff directed me to dig a circle in the Earth—a small, fairly deep circle.

"Can you tell which direction is east?" he asked.

I looked around, suddenly ashamed that I was as good as lost in the woods. I made a guess and pointed.

"Good," Cliff said. "East is the direction where the light comes from each day. So, with the light as your guide, you make the fire the point that fixes the direction east. Then, you walk back and you place the earth you dug out back on the ground. This will be the altar where the pipe and the medicines will sit. In the pit and on the altar you place a small pinch of tobacco—the first medicine—and pray for the humility to complete the ceremony."

Once we'd placed the altar a few paces back from the fire we headed off to a marshy area to gather red willow saplings. Again we said a quiet prayer for each sapling we cut down and offered tobacco to honour its sacrifice.

"The saplings make the frame or the ribs of the lodge. We usually use red willow because the nature of red willow is humility—it always bends but keeps its shape anyway," Walter told me.

"What do you mean, the ribs of the lodge?" I asked, thinking that it was a strange way to describe it.

"Well, the lodge is built round, like the wombs of our mothers. It's round like the Earth. Both of them give us life. So when we put the saplings together we refer to them as the ribs because the womb is sheltered by the ribs. We treat them respectfully, gently, as though they were the ribs of our own mothers. It teaches us to be gentle," he said.

When we found a copse of saplings we laid pinches of tobacco down to thank them for allowing us to make use of them in the ceremony. Then we stripped the branches from the saplings and carried them gently back to the site of the lodge and lay them carefully on the Earth.

Next Cliff pointed out where I should dig small holes that the ends of the saplings would sink into. In each hole I placed a pinch of tobacco and said a prayer for guidance and one of gratitude. It felt strange. My prayers were awkward. Language seemed to fail me when it was called upon to address something other than the everyday. I wondered whether these prayers were being heard. Then, starting from the east, we worked our way around the Four Directions, carefully bending each sapling over, placing each end in one of the small holes. Using bark we stripped from the branches we bound the ribs together while Walter sang a prayer song in his language. It sounded eerie to me, in a cadence and vocabulary I couldn't understand.

"What was that song about?" I asked when he'd finished.

"It was a song asking for the willows to lend us the humility to gain strength from what we are about to do," Cliff said. "Strength comes from humility. Most people get it the other way around, but the lodge teaches us the right flow."

Over the frame we begin placing canvas tarpaulins.

"In the old days they would use hides to do this, but in the modern world there aren't a lot of hides around anymore," Walter said. "The hides represented the Animal People, our greatest teachers, the bringers of the light. As you place the hides on the ribs of the lodge you say a prayer of gratitude for the many teachings of our animal brothers and sisters. Once the frame is covered I want you to take a smudging bowl that is filled with sweet grass, sage, cedar, and tobacco—the four medicines—and walk east to west around the lodge and smudge it with the medicines and offer up a prayer of gratitude and a petition for the teachings needed to help you on your journey. Then put the smudging bowl on the altar at the front of the lodge."

The words felt clumsy, dishonest almost, as I walked around the lodge. I wasn't convinced that I was ready for this.

The strangeness of the smudging bowl, with its pungent smoke and the lightness of the eagle feather they'd given me to pass the smoke over the top of the lodge, felt like the most foreign of tools. I felt awkward using them. Unnatural. I wasn't sure I could get past the fear that, should I fail, I wouldn't measure up as an Indian—though I had only the vaguest sense of what success or failure might mean. But I finished the smudging and laid the bowl and feather lightly on the altar.

We were ready. Cliff's nephew arrived to act as the Fire Keeper—an honoured role in itself. The Fire Keeper's responsibility is to tend to the Grandfathers—and to those who share this ceremony—by having water ready and following the directions of the leader, who on this day would be Walter. We stripped to our skin and washed ourselves in the river that ran by the site. Then we smudged with the medicines. The smudging process is like washing. You bring the smoke from the medicines over your entire body, top to bottom, and Cliff and Walter even smudged the soles of their feet.

"The reason for the washing and the smudging is so that you will be as clean as you were when you arrived here. You're pure," Cliff said. "It's a stripping away of all the worldly things we hide behind—clothing, possessions, jewels, money—and we're completely open to the world again. Completely ourselves, just the way we are. This is humility. The Sweat Lodge is about going back, returning to the Earth, to humility, and your nakedness is a symbol of that humility."

All I could do was look at him. His words seemed so calm, so assured, but all I heard was that I'd be required to forget everything that had helped me to survive, that I'd be helpless once I entered the lodge. That prospect frightened me badly. But I kept up a brave face as we walked around the fire and offered tobacco to the Grandfathers. We walked around the fire, going from east to west, then got down on our hands and knees to crawl inside the lodge.

"You're placing yourself on the Earth and crawling into darkness," Walter said. "The darkness is a symbol of all our doubts and fears. We face them humbly on our hands and knees. It's a good way. Pride keeps us on our feet a lot of times, thinking we can fight them off. We can't."

Walter began to prepare the sacred pipe. We smoked. The pipe felt odd to me, sitting there in the half-darkness, looking towards the open door and the world that looked more inviting right then than it ever had before. I smoked. Deep down I felt proud that I was smoking a ceremonial pipe with other men. But I also felt the creep of fear along my spine.

The Fire Keeper began to bring in the Grandfathers. Walter placed each gently into the pit. Each time, my two friends greeted them—"*Ho, Mishomis,*" meaning "Hello, Grandfather." When the proper number of Grandfathers for the first round of the ceremony were present Walter signalled the Fire Keeper to close the door of the lodge.

This was darkness. Pure, utter, and complete. There was no light at all except for the red glow of the Grandfathers. The smoke from the pipe and the burning sweet grass, cedar, and sage burned my eyes and I felt choked and unable to breathe. I was afraid. A part of me recognized this darkness. It was the darkness I had felt inside me all my life. Now, here I was, sitting in its very middle, naked, powerless, and feeling very, very small. I concentrated on the symbol of the womb that my friends had talked about. I was in the womb of my birth mother and I was in the womb of the Great Mother, Mother Earth, and for a moment that thought calmed me. But when Walter and Cliff started to sing, all comfort disappeared.

Then came the first splash of water on the Grandfathers. There was a loud hiss as the water was transformed into steam. The heat in the lodge rose sharply. I could feel it settle over every part of my body like a sheet of fire. More water was splashed onto the rocks and the heat became searing. My lungs felt scalded. Sweat coursed down my face into the corners of my eyes and burned them. My hair felt so dry and brittle that I was afraid it would burst into flame. I brushed sweat from my face and neck onto my hair to wet it down as the heat grew more and more intense—as did the singing and chanting. The prayers continued as more and more water was splashed. The intensity in the lodge was frightening. I found myself beginning to pray. I prayed like I never had before, talking, beseeching, moaning, and crying words I never thought I would say. I asked for things like strength, courage, faith, and outright help from the power of Creation to protect me and see me through. I asked for forgiveness for all the things I suddenly knew were wrong. I asked for help to try and live a different way.

One of my friends had a rattle now and was shaking it in time with his singing. The stream of sweat coursing down my body was like all the tears I had ever wanted to shed. I could feel the grief, anger, fear, jealousy, envy, pride, guilt, and shame seep out of every pore, every ounce of my being, and that's when the real tears began to follow them down my chest. I heaved great sobbing bunches of them. They coursed down the front of my body in what felt like waves and I felt washed in the great flood of my experiences. I was a little boy. I was a teenager. I was a young man. I was me. And in each I felt the burn of bitterness and shame, smelled the stink of fear, and tasted the rancid breath of loneliness. It felt great to cry and wail. It was a release. Then, when it seemed like the heat and the energy in the lodge could climb no higher, Walter called for the Fire Keeper to open the door.

This was the coming of the Light.

From the darkness, heat, and discomfort, I was instantly transported to a world of light, cool air, and ease. The burdens, so cumbersome in the darkness, were *light*-ened. I sat there, breathing deeply, drinking the cool air into the very depths of my spirit. All I could think and feel was gratitude. The only thoughts I could hold onto were those concerned with the difficulty of the ceremony, of this ritual journey, and how the light represented the easing of that difficulty. We laughed now as we relaxed in the coolness and light. Walter told a few funny stories about Sweat Lodge ceremonies he'd been to in the past and the laughter felt good. My heart felt alive inside my chest. My mind was clear.

Then the signal was given for the door to be closed and we were thrown into darkness again. Three more times I would be plunged back into darkness to feel the hardship, to release the effects of my history, my choices, my hurts, wounds, scars, secrets, and self-harm. Three more times I would confront myself in all humility. Each time the door closed I was filled with fear. I swore I could see things move in the darkness. I saw faces in the glow of the rocks. I saw the image of a bear, a great black bear, form where the roof of the lodge should have been. It hung there for an instant, then dissolved. During the third round I heard the frantic flapping of the wings of a great bird over and around me. All of it frightened me. By the fourth round I could feel myself sapped of all energy and I had to lie down upon the floor of the lodge and press my face as close as I could to the earth. It felt cooler there. I lay there spent, crying in shallower gasps, my fingers curled into the soft earth. When the door was opened for the fourth and final time and I crawled out of the lodge and back into the world, I felt lessened and enlarged at the same time.

There was a feast afterwards at Walter's home. Thankful prayers were said. When I offered mine the words didn't feel as strange and awkward as they had earlier in the day. The food, water and juices tasted more wonderful than anything I had ever had and I could feel my body sing with the acceptance of their goodness. I was tired but energized and when the time came to say "farewell" I did so with a heart brimming with well-being, kinship, and harmony.

I don't know how long that feeling lasted once I went back into my regular life. I do know that I felt a deep sense of honour over being included. I also felt a touch of pride in myself for completing the entire journey that day. I had endured. I had defeated the urge to quit, and in the process I had heard myself say, in the sweltering darkness of the Sweat Lodge, things I had never thought I would ever say.

"This is healing," Walter said. "This is spiritual. You learn that the lesson of humility is that when you give away, surrender, you receive in equal or greater measure. You have surrendered yourself and increased yourself on this journey. You have brought the Light into your world."

An Ojibway child was born in a small village. He was very different from any other baby that had ever been born there. This child, this boy, was born with a face that was twisted and misshapen. His body was bent and crooked and he could not walk or move about like the other children. All the people felt great pity for this child, and even though they honoured him and protected him as they did the others, they never believed the boy would be anything but a burden to them.

But his mother and father loved him very much. When they looked at him they did not see a misshapen body or twisted face. Instead, what they saw was a beautiful baby boy who was a great gift to them. They named him Wass-co-nah-shpee-ming—Light in the Sky. To his parents the boy shone like a great, bright light in the sky of their lives and they adored him.

As he grew, it became apparent that he could not talk like the other children. His throat was twisted like the rest of his body and when he tried to say anything it always came out a throttled croak. When they heard these strange noises coming from the boy some of the people laughed, some of the people cried, and some felt ashamed, but no one except his parents sat down and tried to talk with him. He grew excited when they did. His eyes got large and his crooked arms waved about and he croaked happily.

When the other people heard these sounds they scuttled off quickly to another part of the village. They believed the boy was stupid. They believed his mind was as badly made as his body. But his parents had hope, and they encouraged him to talk even more, and more loudly, too. When he did, the others became even more ashamed and embarrassed.

Light in the Sky knew what he wanted to say. He could feel the words in his body. He could feel them in his heart, could feel them trying to work their way upwards through his lungs to his neck, his throat, his mouth, but his tongue betrayed him. And some of the people laughed, some of the people cried, and some felt ashamed. But no one sat down and tried to talk to him.

As he grew older he was cast out by the other children. They did not try to include him in their games and he contented himself with lurching about on his crutch amongst the trees, watching the magnificent world around him. He wanted very badly to express the joy he felt in the wonders of the world, but he could not. Still, it did not stop him from heading out each day to watch the world and learn even more about its ways. He learned to stand very quietly and respectfully amidst the trees, rivers, and rocks. He learned to feel a part of all of it. Whenever he went out he could feel the words forming in his chest like a great cloud ready to rain blessings on all that he saw. But the words would never come and Wass-co-nah-shpee-ming was sad.

His parents often spoke with the wise woman of the village. They told her of the great love and affection they held for their son. They told her of the dreams they nursed for him and the sadness that came when they realized that he might never achieve them. The old woman was touched deeply by their honest love.

"He speaks a language of his own," the old woman said. "All of us need to learn how to use our ears again in order to hear it. Someday we will."

When his parents pressed the old woman for more details, for more reassurance, she smiled and said simply, "Be patient."

They were patient a long time. In the summer of the year that Light in the Sky was ten, a great drought descended on the land. There was no rain for months. The forest grew dry and the waters grew shallow and warm. Animals and fish were rarely seen and the berries were skimpy and thin. The people worried. With the coming of the winter months they would need great supplies of meat, dried berries, and fish. They prayed and prayed to Gitchee Manitou for the Thunderbirds to bring the rain they so desperately needed.

But none came. Some of the men had travelled by canoe to the furthest reaches of their territory but they returned with nothing. The drought seemed to have withered everything. All around him Wass-co-nah-shpee-ming could see and feel the cloud of worry that spread amongst the people. When he stood amongst the trees he felt a great silence. This silence did not frighten him, though. It seemed to be a pause in the flow of energy he felt there, like the rest that comes between breaths. But he couldn't tell anyone. The words would not form.

One night, unable to sleep, Light in the Sky crept from his family's wigwam. It was a clear, hot night and he felt like wading in the shallows to cool his feet. As he hitched his way along the narrow path that led to the lake he thought about the people and the way worry had fallen upon them. It was a huge weight. He could feel its heft in the way people spoke to each other these days. He could see it in the pinched way their faces moved, how forced their smiles were. It saddened him. He wished for a return of the bubbly joy and humour he loved so much about them.

He waded slowly into the water. Above him the moon shone bright and full, throwing deep shadows across the land. He raised his face to it, closed his eyes, and said a silent prayer for the people. The water lapped at his ankles and he felt calm, peaceful and unafraid. He kept his eyes closed and imagined that he was the Moon, hanging so full and silent above the Earth. From there he could see everything. He felt like a protective brother watching over his people and the land.

Suddenly, Wass-co-nah-shpee-ming heard a sound. It seemed to come from the Earth itself and rose upwards into the sky like the sudden grey explosion of a heron from the trees. Then it was gone. He opened his eyes and looked about him. All he could see was bush and trees and the Moon upon the water. Across the small lake a huge cliff rose, and he looked over at it. The sound came again. It was high and shrill. Within its piercing trill was a loneliness he recognized, but there was also a note of praise, of jubilation and freedom he recognized, too. It was captivating. He closed his eyes again and raised his face to the Moon as though the very act could summon the sound. It did.

When he heard it, Light in the Sky opened his eyes and looked at the cliff across the lake, for that seemed to be where the sound was coming from. There, high on the cliff raising his snout to the Moon, was Myeengun, the Wolf. He had never seen Myeengun before or heard his call, but he'd heard stories. The Wolf was a very respected animal amongst the people and Wass-co-nah-shpee-ming felt honoured to be standing in the water watching and listening as Myeengun sang his song to the Moon. He thought that the Wolf must be on a journey to find food for *his* people, too, and when he heard his song again he could sense Myeengun's desire to provide for his family. He could sense his worry. He could sense his love. He could sense that Myeengun felt the same high regard for his people that Wass-co-nah-shpee-ming felt for his own, so that when Myeengun raised his voice to the Moon again, Light in the Sky raised *his* voice, too.

"Ow-ooo ooo-ooo-ooo," said the Wolf.

"Ow-guh-guh-guh," replied Wass-co-nah-shpee-ming.

Time and time again Myeengun called, and time and time again Light in the Sky tried to imitate the voice. But his throat would not move in the right way. The notes were strangled in his throat. Still, each time Myeengun called, the more desperately he tried to respond. The Wolf's call was like a prayer and Light in the Sky wanted more than anything in the world to echo that prayer. He wanted his voice to carry his love, compassion, concern, and respect for his people upwards to the Moon, to the universe, to the invisible.

Gradually, slowly, his voice changed. His throat stretched. The desire he felt in his heart began to slide upwards through his lungs to his throat, his tongue, and into his mouth.

"Ow-ooo-ooo-ooo," said Myeengun.

"Ow-ooo-ooo-ooo," replied Wass-co-nah-shpee-ming.

There was silence. Then, slowly, Myeengun raised his voice again, and slowly Wass-co-nah-shpee-ming replied. A pause. Silence. And then, again and again and again, Myeengun sang out to the Moon and each time Light in the Sky answered. The boy's heart was filled with incredible joy. This was an experience he had never imagined. Here was another being who heard him, spoke with him, felt his words and understood him. Wass-co-nah-shpee-ming felt like his heart would burst with the sheer joy of it.

Then, as mysteriously as he'd arrived, Myeengun was gone. Wass-co-nah-shpee-ming stood in the shallow water and looked upwards at the Moon that still hung fat and silent and watchful over everything. His heart was light and he raised his face to the heavens and called out on his own, "Ow-ooo-ooo-ooo, ow-ooo-ooo-ooo!" Every bit of joy, celebration, praise, love, and honour that he felt welling up inside him went into that call, and when its last note faded off into the air he turned and hitched his way back up the trail to his family's wigwam and slept.

The people were excited over the appearance of the Wolf. They took it as a good sign and for a few days their hearts were light. But when the drought continued and their bellies continued to feel that deep hunger they sank into worry again. Wass-co-nah-shpee-ming watched this happen and was saddened. There was nothing he could say, even though every fibre of his being called out to his people to have hope, to believe that Myeengun did in fact come to bring a message to them, to stay strong within themselves.

Each night he crept out of his wigwam and went to the lake to sing his song to the universe. Each night he thought about his people, his mother and father, his friends, and he put every ounce of care and concern and love for them into his voice. His song was pure. It was a prayer and he felt every word.

The people thought it was Myeengun they heard those nights and they could not figure out why the Wolf was staying so close to them.

"Maybe to pick our bones when we drop from starvation," someone said.

"Or maybe he's crying for us because there is no relief in sight," said another.

"Or maybe he's teaching us a mourning song," said someone else.

Only Wass-co-nah-shpee-ming knew the truth but he could not tell anyone. Every night he went to the lake and sang his prayer song to the universe. Every night he felt the motions of love in his heart and every night he sang that love to the stars. His voice grew stronger.

The drought continued and the people grew tired. Soon there were arguments and shouting around the campfires, and people began to hoard scraps of food rather than share as they were accustomed to. Jealousy and judgement were everywhere. It began to seem as though someone would die from the hunger. Bitterness grew among them.

One night a loud argument erupted. One family that had some food was trying to keep it away from another family going without. Accusations and threats were shouted. A fight started and soon everyone was involved. People were invading other wigwams, tossing things around in attempts to find food they were certain was secreted away somewhere. The entire village was in an uproar and everyone was angry.

Suddenly the people heard a mournful cry raised up among them. It was Myeengun's voice, but it was coming from Wass-co-nah-shpee-ming. He stood square in the middle of the village with his face raised up to the universe and sang the song of the Wolf. It was pure and strong and loud. Everyone stopped their running about and turned to see this magic.

"Ow-ooo-ooo-ooo," sang Light in the Sky. "Ow-ow-ow-ooo!"

Slowly everyone walked towards the middle of the village and stood in a big circle around the bent and twisted boy who sang so beautifully in the night. He sang and sang and sang. When he was finished he looked around at the great circle of his people and tears shone on his face. It saddened him so much to see them fight amongst themselves and forget the teachings of sharing and community they lived by. He walked around that circle and took each person's face in his small crooked hands and looked deeply into every pair of eyes. There was not a single member of that village who did not feel the message that Wass-co-nah-shpee-ming's eyes carried that night. Not one member of that tribal family was not touched by the depth of the love and concern they felt flowing from that small crooked boy. Every person felt spoken to. Comforted. Loved.

When he'd completed the circle and looked into every face, Light in the Sky moved into the centre of the village again. He motioned his parents over to join him and when they did he took their hands in his own, raised his face to the sky again, and sang. His mother and father were very proud and they cried openly in love for their son whose voice rang so clearly over everything.

"Ow-ow-ow-ooo!" he sang. "Ow-ow-ow-ooo!"

Then, someone gasped and pointed to the east. There, above the treetops, the Moon was rising full and round and orange against the night. As Wass-co-nah-shpee-ming's song continued the Moon rose higher and higher into the sky. And then, as if that magic weren't enough, the people heard another voice raised up in song to mingle with the boy's. Myeengun. Together the boy and the Wolf welcomed the Moon back to the sky. Together they praised Creation for its blessings, its mysteries, its guidance. Together they sang a song that reminded the people of all the teachings the drought had forced them to forget.

They began to cry. They poured out all their hurt and disappointment. They poured out their anger, resentment, jealousy, fear, and indifference. They poured out their love and concern for each other. The Wolf song continued and the people felt their energy returning, felt their faith rekindled, and their belief in the kindness of Creation take hold again.

When they opened their eyes again they saw a wondrous sight. Bathed in the silver glow of the moonlight was Wass-co-nah-shpee-ming. But it was not the bent and twisted boy they'd known all their lives. Instead, in his place stood a beautiful, straight, strong youth with eyes that shone like the Moon itself. He was radiant and perfect. Beyond them the people heard Myeengun's relatives join him in song. A chorus of wolves raised their songs to the Moon, and in their shrill keening Wass-co-nah-shpee-ming walked around the circle of the village again and looked into every face. Not a person did not cry in joy and awe at the beauty of this youth or the pure, splendid light of love they saw in his eyes. Not a person felt unheard, unspoken to, unloved.

And when he'd made his way around and faced his parents again, the Wolf song grew louder and louder. Wass-co-nah-shpee-ming looked adoringly at the two people who had loved him all his life and celebrated the beauty they had known he carried within him. He reached out and touched them and then, as the Wolf song rose and fell, a wonderful thing happened. He began to glow, silvery, ghostly, like the light of the Moon, and as he spread his arms in celebration of the song that filled the night he began to float upwards and upwards away from them. As the people watched in humble awe Wass-co-nah-shpee-ming rose higher and higher and higher until finally they saw him float right up into the face of the Moon.

And suddenly the Wolf song died away.

Silence. A pause, and then, very quietly in the distance, the people heard the rumble of thunder. The air cooled suddenly, and against the horizon they could see the edges of rain clouds scuttling towards them. The clouds moved in very quickly and surrounded the Moon where Wass-co-nah-shpee-ming had settled. When the clouds were thick with the promise of rain they blanketed the Moon and its light winked out just as the first wet thick drops of rain began to fall.

The people cried in joy and celebration. They danced amongst the raindrops. They danced and danced and danced, grateful for the rain, for Light in the Sky and the magic they had seen. It rained for four days and after that the berries flourished, the fish returned to their pools, and game became plentiful again. When winter came the people had more than enough to see them through the cold months. And each of those cold winter months brought a brilliant silver moon to the sky and the people sang in celebration of the boy who had reminded them that faith would always see them through the toughest of times, that feeding the spirit was as important as feeding the body, and that they needed each other for survival.

But there were two who were confused, who felt a deep sense of loss for their son. Wass-co-nah-shpee-ming's parents went to see the wise woman. They wanted to know why this had happened. As grateful as they were for the events of the past summer they wanted to know why their son could not stay with them, why he needed to live in the Moon.

"All of his life your son felt the words he wanted to speak. He felt them in his heart, in his spirit. He knew them as truth and he wanted to share this truth more than he wanted anything in the world. He wanted to speak the language of his heart. Myeengun gave him the gift of song and he found his voice. When he did, he put all of his love, compassion, forgiveness, loyalty, kindness, truth, and wisdom into it and the universe chose to honour him for that. He lives in the Moon to remind us always of the lesson he was sent to carry to us," the wise woman said.

"What lesson is that?" his parents asked.

The wise one smiled kindly. "That only with the heart can we truly speak, and only with the heart can we find and become who and what we were created to be. That is Wass-co-nah-shpee-ming's gift to us all."

The night was deep and dark. High above me the stars seemed far brighter than they ever had and I saw shadows thrown by their intensity. Memories of the Sweat Lodge had made me very thirsty and I slaked that thirst with two huge gulps from the canteen. That ceremony had been a great gift. For a short time after that first Sweat Lodge I felt that anything was possible and I dove into my life wholeheartedly.

But I still carried around the old feelings of shame, hurt, and unworthiness. Despite everything that was given to me I still held onto those old beliefs. I could not shake them loose no matter how desperately I desired to. I still chose to believe that I did not belong, did not fit, and did not deserve all the good that our way and our people offered me. They could not fix me. They could not heal me. They could not take away the great hurts and bruises inside me. I felt that if my people knew that I had been to jail numerous times, if they knew that I had lied, cheated, and stole, that I had hurt a great many people, they would not welcome me into their circle. So I did the only thing that I knew how to do: I hid myself and my feelings. When those feelings got to be too much to bear, I drank again.

I drank a lot through those next years. Even though I started to find success in my work, even though I was a participant at ceremonies, even though I appeared proud, strong, and capable, I felt none of that. I always felt like a liar, a fraud, a con. I was unable to forgive myself for the way I had lived my life, for the choices I had made, and my inability to forgive myself left only blame in its place. So I blamed other people. I blamed foster homes, adoption, the white man, society, history, government, sexism, racism—and I blamed myself. It always came back to my own unworthiness, the fact that I was unlovable, unwanted, a failure. And so I drank. I'd stay sober for months at a time but always the feelings arose and I would have to drink to kill them. I would have to, despite the experience of the Sweat Lodge.

When I drank again after being sober for a long period the guilt I felt was unbearable. I felt guilty that I was disrespecting the teachings, guilty that I wasn't living the way I knew was the way to live, and guilty that I was weak and afraid. So I drank even more. When it got so bad that I was sick from drinking, shaking, sweating, vomiting, seeing things, hearing things, I drank so I wouldn't be sick and wound up drunk again. Then I would lie, cheat, and steal all over again and the guilt would continue. And so would that circle of pain.

I was in that vicious cycle a long time. Time and again I would get sober and do something positive. Time and again I would have people in my life who were there only to help me. Time and again the way was offered me, and I came close to grabbing for it sometimes. But fear always held me back. Always. I was afraid that if I made the journey to inside all I would find was the liar, cheat, and thief I knew I was. I was afraid that I would discover the me I was always afraid existed. So I faked it. I became what a lot of unhealed Native people become. I became an Indian of convenience.

An Indian of convenience is an Indian who knows of the teachings and the way, but doesn't *really* know them. An Indian of convenience picks the parts of our teachings and of our way that don't cost too much in terms of sacrifice and uses them. Displays them. An Indian of convenience chooses to display attitude over knowledge, appearances over humility, and cultural activities over traditional teachings and living. Mostly though, an Indian of convenience is a person who gives the impression of belonging, fitting, knowing, and being but who hasn't found the courage to begin the greatest of all journeys: the journey to inside.

That's who I was for a long time. I had the hair, the dances, the drumming, the clothes, the head knowledge and the skill to speak of all of it, and the greater skill to write of it, but that's all I had. I had the outside down pat but my insides, where I really lived, were in turmoil, pain, and confusion and they always got me drunk, always drove the people who cared for me from my life, always helped me create more guilt. My working life was becoming a success, I'd been involved with several beautiful, talented women who genuinely cared for me, the Native community was welcoming and generous, and I had money in the bank. But it seemed that nothing was ever enough to ease my pain. Nothing.

As I watched the sky and thought about the agony I'd endured as a young man searching for himself, the agony of the Sweat Lodge ritual, the agony of my alcoholism, and the agony of four days of solitude on a ledge facing the mountains, I realized that I had never known the most crucial of teachings: that nothing in the world was ever going to be enough for me until I was enough for me.

I smiled at that. So clear, so simple, so true.

The night sky was a huge purple bowl of sky dotted with the icy points of stars. And as I sat there drinking it all in I thought about how those stars represented so many possible worlds. I wondered if there were travellers like me in each of those worlds, wanderers, nomads, who might have been graced with a friend like John, a night like this and a universe that felt close enough to touch, so that finally, sometime before sleep grabbed me in comforting arms, I imagined I could see a rover on one of those worlds, sitting on the same kind of hill on the same kind of night, on the same search as I was. I waved to him. Wished him well. Then, as sleep descended, I imagined him waving back. I smiled.

## IV

## WISDOM

In my dream I was a young boy again. The land was exactly as I remembered, thick with bush and rock and water. The light of the sun reflected off all those rivers and lakes so that finally the light I moved through was a mercurial silver sliding upwards into gold, an infinite, nurturing light. And I was running. Above me was the hard blue helmet of the sky and around me the trees like crooked fingers raised upwards in praise. Even the rocks lay lodged in the breast of the Earth like hymns. I was naked—stark naked—except for a pair of big black gumboots that I was struggling not to run completely out of. The tops of those big boots slapped against my thighs, and behind me I could hear the exaggerated thump of feet in hot pursuit. I was laughing. Ahead of me was the glitter of a lake and as I burst from the trees onto a platform of rock the sun blinded me for an instant.

At that moment I was grabbed from behind and lifted into the air. I felt strong arms enfold me and there was a wild flail of hair against my face. It smelled of wood smoke and I laughed as I lifted a hand to part it from my face.

Only it wasn't hair.

It was a curtain. A thick curtain hung in front of a window to block off light. As I parted it the sunlight streaming into the room was hard and I squinted against it. When my eyes adjusted I was looking out at a playground. There were hundreds of children there, running, playing, laughing. It seemed a happy enough scene, but as I scanned it my gaze came to rest on one small child alone in a sandbox at the far edge of the lot. He was playing with a tiny red truck, concentrating very hard at moving piles of sand and oblivious to the scurrying throng around him. Just then the recess bell rang and he looked up. It was me. It was me at six or seven years old—small, crew cut, thick glasses, with baggy clothes, oversized to grow into. The children all raced towards the school and I walked slowly, obediently, behind them. The laughter and happy chatter began to fade into silence. As I watched myself as a little boy move towards the building, all the world receded into a thick silence until finally I could see only the small boy moving evenly towards the waiting school. I couldn't stand it. I threw open the window and stepped through it into the playground.

Only it wasn't a playground.

It was a laneway. Flat, narrow and gravelled, it meandered through a brown landscape, furrowed and even as a table. There were few trees, skinny, leafless, and stunted. There was a moon hovering over everything and I walked in shadow. I felt a great sadness within myself and the salty taste of tears at the back of my tongue. Ahead of me was a house. It stood alone in a great field and every window was ablaze with light. The closer I got to that house the more the weight of sadness slowed me down. I heard my footsteps fall in even measure like a drum being thumped at a funereal tempo. When I got to the door of that house it opened and I heard a voice saying, "It's about time. How long did you expect us to wait for you?" I swallowed hard and stepped through the doorway and into the house.

Only it wasn't a house.

It was a powwow ground. There were hundreds of people sitting in a huge circle, within which there were many dancers shuffling clockwise to the heavy beat of a drum and the shrill wail of singers who sat under an arbour of cedar boughs in the very middle of that great circle. The dancers were a glorious sight. They wore every colour of the rainbow and their regalia shook and shimmered. Its brilliance rivalled that of the sun. Here an old man in elaborately beaded buckskin. There a young girl in a long dress adorned with jingling metal cones. Behind her a young man bedecked with long skirts of gold yarn and a headpiece of porcupine quills and fur. Old women in simpler dresses, carrying eagle feather fans, were followed by middle-aged men with eagle feather bustles on their backs, great breastplates of deer bone and faces painted in bold patterns. Everyone, it seemed, was dressed in celebration. Then, one by one as they danced past me, they motioned for me to join them. I felt fear. But as that long line of dancers passed I began to feel people closing in behind me. Many hands pressed gently against my back and I was eased outwards into the dancing area.

My feet began to move, seeking out the tempo of the drum. But as I moved I felt a terrible weight on my body. I wanted to move faster, to join that drum and the voices of the singers, but gravity worked against me. I strained against the pressure and as I collapsed my face into a grimace of agony I caught a reflection of myself in one of the small mirrors one of the dancers had mounted on his shield. I wasn't dressed ceremonially. I was in rags that fluttered around me.

In the mirror I saw remnants of material I recognized. There was the harsh blue of prison shirts; beside it, the lime green of the trousers I had worn to school the first day at Dalewood; next to that the grey silk of a suit I'd once owned; there was a swatch of faded denim, a flag of black leather, and a strip of T-shirt with "Rick's a drunk" emblazoned on it. I stopped where I was and I felt the burning desire to flee. I felt shame and anger that my regalia was that of a wanderer who'd never found a home, a tribe, or a family. Everyone could see how my outfit reflected who I was—and who I had never been.

I turned towards the people seated around the dancing area, looking for an opening, a place to run through. As I did, the beat of the drum slowed and the voices of the singers moved into a more solemn cadence. The dancers surrounded me. They looked at me, and in their eyes I saw sorrow and empathy. They began to dance slowly around me and as they passed, one by one, they tore off the strips of material I was dressed in. I felt the weight lessen as the rags fell away. I stood there unable to move until finally I felt naked. But strangely there was no shame in my nakedness. Instead, I felt comforted, and as I watched them an old man began to walk towards me. He was carrying a blanket. The closer he came the more I could see the light in his eyes. It was a brilliant light, one that spoke of knowledge and healing. As he got closer he began to open that blanket. It was purple, a deep, deep purple, and at its centre was a huge star pattern done in an orange—more rust than tangerine. When he reached me he opened his arms wide and wrapped me in that blanket. It felt smooth, worn with age, comfortable and safe. I grasped its edges and pulled it closer around me. Then he held out a pipe. It looked ancient. Fragile, but very strong. I felt embarrassed because I'd been told how sacred a pipe was to my people and I felt undeserving of handling it. But the old man stood there, imploring me with his eyes to take the pipe. I did. When I looked at that old man the light in his eyes shone clearly, strongly, and I squinted them closed. When I opened them again the light shone brightly in my eyes. I wanted to smile at that old man.

Only it wasn't the old man.

It was the sun.

The morning was bright and clear and around me I could hear the sounds of the birds, squirrels, and chipmunks busy with their lives. I rubbed the sleep from my eyes and sat up. The effect of being removed from the dream so suddenly was confusing. The real world seemed strange and foreign. It took a while to adjust to being awake and there was a part of me that wanted to sink back into sleep again and get back to the dream. Instead, I took a swallow of water and began to think about my vision and the three days I'd spent on that hill.

I wasn't afraid anymore. Where shadow had seemed so mysterious and threatening mere hours before it was only shadow now—a part of the pattern, just like I was. The animals I could hear around me weren't predatory, nor were they prey; they were friends and neighbours now. Thinking of that, I thought about the people in that powwow ground in my dream. They'd been as welcoming as the first traditional Native people I'd met when I was twenty-four. I laughed. If I'd only known then how welcome I was, how the rags of my life meant nothing to them at all, that they were willing to help me learn to dress in something more real and healing than I'd ever worn, maybe I would have grown up then. Maybe I could have spared myself the years of agony between then and now. Those people had known what the word "community" meant because they had lived it—and they'd been taught it by ones who knew by living too.

I thought about the pipe the old man in my dream had given me. When I had first seen one all those years ago it had frightened me, because of all the bunk and hogwash I'd come to believe that a pipe represented: pagan worship, bad medicine, something akin to voodoo. But it was never any of that. The pipe had always been about belonging, about community, about unity. Sitting on the hill on that bright, clear morning, feeling a perfect fit with everything that surrounded me, I thought about what I'd been taught about the pipe.

John and I were sitting on the floor of his living room, preparing to go on a trip to take part in a special ceremony in Montana. He showed me how to wrap all of the articles he would need and I was very deliberate in following his instructions. Finally, he took an old elk hide pouch from the cloth it was wrapped in. It was adorned with elaborate floral beadwork and it was beautiful.

"This was a gift from the man who taught me," John said. "It was given to him by his grandfather, so who knows how old it is. It's pretty old, though."

"What is it?" I asked.

"It's a pipe bag. It's the womb that carries my pipe. Keeps it safe. Keeps it strong," he said.

"There's a peace pipe in there?" I asked in awe.

"Well, there's a pipe in here," he said. "I'm not so sure it's a peace pipe. But it's a pipe."

"Aren't they called peace pipes?"

He leaned back on his arms and set the pipe bag on the floor in front of him. Looking at me, he smiled. "That's what most people think. Seems like everyone when they first come around have the idea that our pipes are peace pipes. Guess maybe they get to that, but it's not what they were created to be."

He went on to explain a lot to me.

"When settler people came to this country they saw our people sitting in a circle on the ground and smoking a 'peace pipe.' They called it this because smoking the pipe always went before the good talk and neighbourliness our ancestors displayed, so the assumption that the pipe was intended for 'peace' was an easy one to make. But we never called it that. For us it was a 'unity pipe.'"

"Isn't that kind of the same thing, though?" I asked.

He smiled. "Well, unity means 'a coming together.' We behaved really solemnly around the pipe and I guess the newcomers thought we regarded peace as a sacred thing. But they missed the point. We regard *unity* as sacred. When unity happens, peace is a result. Unity results in all sorts of other things, too—things like equality, respect, dignity, truth, wisdom, kindness, love, honesty, and honour. When these come about, then—and only then—does peace come about.

Our old people understood and taught this, so that the pipe was about joining, coming together, a bonding of very sacred and spiritual forces and energies. It was a unity pipe."

"But it's still sacred?" I asked.

"Oh, yes," John said. "The pipe is very sacred. It's the most powerful tool we have for talking with the Creator and our spirit helpers. There are songs to be sung and prayers to be offered by the pipe carrier. It takes many years to learn all of these songs and petitions."

"Petitions?" I asked. "You mean like a paper you get people to sign to show they're behind something?"

"No," he said. "A petition is a humble asking. It's the voice of the people, through the pipe, for the things in life that are vital to us—things like security or safety, sufficiency, or enough to eat, wisdom, or the ability to see truth, reverence for life, a kind heart, and humility. The reason it takes so long to learn all the songs and petitions is because you gotta be pretty humble to humbly ask on behalf of other people. Gotta be pretty humble to be the one that does that without getting all puffed up with importance. It's a hard thing for a human being to learn. Takes a long time."

"Can anybody learn?"

He crossed his legs and placed the pipe bag in his lap. "These days there's lots of pipe carriers. When I was learning these things finding a pipe carrier took a lot of effort. There weren't many because the elders who carried the old pipes were very careful in choosing their helpers, the ones who would receive the teachings. Helpers had to prove themselves as dedicated, spiritually honest, kind, and humble before they began to be taught. Then, over time, they would be introduced to the pipe. The pipe teachings took years to learn. Along the way the helper was always being studied for their readiness to become a pipe carrier.

"Nowadays there's pipes and pipe carriers everywhere. That's not such a good thing because people learn the easiest part of the responsibility—the words and motions—but not many sacrifice the time and comfort to learn the humility. The pipe's all about humility. Without humility the pipe is just wood and stone."

Gently, slowly, John opened the pipe bag. I watched in rapt fascination. The room seemed to grow still and silent around us and John's movements seemed to take forever. On the floor in front of him now were two wrapped objects.

"There's two parts to the pipe and they represent the two streams of life. First, there's the bowl."

John carefully unwrapped one of the objects and held it up with both hands for me to see. It was a rust-red-coloured piece of stone carved into a deep bowl at the top and a short bored shaft beneath.

"This is the bowl, made and carved from stone. It's not just any stone. This stone comes from a sacred place and only those who have learned enough pipe teachings can go there to get it. We call it pipestone."

Then he unwrapped the second part. It was a long, narrow pale-brown piece of wood with some scrollwork along its length.

"This is the stem, made and carved from wood. There's different kinds of wood used in stem making but this one is birch—the talking tree. Birch is what we Ojibway people used to make our teaching scrolls.

"Neither part is more important than the other. They are each as 'sacred' as the other. The first quality of a pipe and its first teaching is equality or balance."

"What does that mean exactly?" I asked.

"When things are in balance there's no struggle, no confusion, no judgement, only harmony. Harmony is a word that's used a lot in talk about our ways. It means 'all things true together.'"

"I don't get it," I said. As much as I wanted to learn about these things, all the talk of qualities and spirituality was going over my head. I felt confused and frightened.

John smiled again. "Sometimes we get all carried away with gettin' what we think's owed us, what we deserve. So we struggle really hard to get above things, to get above where other people are. When we do that we forget about equality. We forget that we are all children of one Creator and therefore all equal. The pipe reminds us of its first teaching—that we are all equal, that we were all created exactly the same. We all carry the same gifts within us. We all have the same hungers. We all crave the same joys. The pipe reminds us of that.

"The bowl represents spirituality or 'living from the heart.' When you live from the heart you see the Creator in everything and everybody. When you live from the heart you feel truth before you understand truth. The bowl, and the stone it's made of, reminds us that spirituality, and the faith that comes from it, lasts forever. It's eternal, like the rocks, the mountains, the backbone of Mother Earth. Faith means 'choosing to believe' and the bowl asks us to choose to believe in Creation and its teachings."

"Wow," I said quietly. "What about the stem?"

"The stem represents life—all things that grow. Sometimes a pipe has an animal skin wrapped around the stem, or feathers or grasses. They serve to remind us of the different lives around us and that we are all the same. Unlike the stone of the bowl, the wooden stem is fragile—it can be chipped or broken, it might rot or decay—and it reminds us that life is fragile. It reminds us that life will eventually end. This is where the most vital teaching is."

"There's more?" I asked, my head already reeling with the depth of what John was giving me.

"See how each part of the pipe is wrapped separately from the other?"

I nodded.

"Well, they're kept apart until songs are sung and prayers offered for each of them. The reason is that both spirituality and life need to be honoured. They need to be recognized for the power they each carry. Separately. The prayers offered for the bowl and the stem are very old because they have been the foundation of our way for a long time. When the prayers are finished the elder, or pipe carrier, unwraps each element. They are smudged with sweet grass, tobacco, and sage so they are clean, pure, and free of anything that might block their ability to carry prayers and petitions. Then they are joined, and this is the reason why a pipe ceremony is so solemn: the moment when the bowl and stem are joined, when unity is achieved, is the most powerful teaching our people have."

"What teaching is that?" I asked.

"That the joining of life to spirituality is the most sacred joining."

John smoked a cigarette while I stared out the window and considered all of this. At that time I equated spirituality with religion and I sure didn't want much to do with any religion. Still, being Indian meant following these teachings and I wanted to try this way, even though I was sure that it would prove impossible for me.

"Isn't it hard, though? I mean, it all sounds really good and you make it sound like we all kind of get led to living as the pipe teaches. But what about the world? Getting along in the world is tough. I had to fight just to get by lots of times and if I'd stopped to try and be spiritual through any of it I probably would have died." I was amazed how easily that all flowed out of me.

"Living life spiritually isn't as tough a thing as it sounds—or as people make it out to be," John said. "Most times people make it sound hard because it's the opposite of what their minds tell them life should be like. That's the difference. To live spiritually means to be on the look out for things our spirit *desires*. Things like serenity or peace, love, truth, harmony, and reverence for life—stuff that lasts forever.

"To live for our mind means bein' on the lookout for the

things our heads tell us we *need*. Things like security, possessions, acceptance, and gain—stuff that fades.

"A desire pushes us forwards and a need holds us back. So when we join the act of living every day to the desires of our spirit it is a sacred moment, a sacred joining, and the only real goal we need to work for. If that was all the pipe had to teach us, or to symbolize for us, it would be a very great thing. But there is more."

I groaned. "I don't think I can take any more. Just thinking over all of this is going to give me a major headache!"

John laughed. "Yeah. I guess it would. But you don't have to think about it all at once. Take a part of it and consider that for a while. Then, take another part. The trick is in wanting to come back to the teachings all the time to learn more. That's the hard part—being willing to come back to it."

"Okay, okay," I said, also laughing now. "I have one tiny little bit of head space left. What else is there?"

"Well, the bowl of the pipe also symbolizes the spirit of the woman. It's round like the womb in our mother's belly. Of all the creatures in Creation, only the female is capable of giving life, only she has life-giving energy. When she carried us she gave us qualities that only a woman can give— gentleness, humour, compassion, empathy, wisdom, and reverence for life—so that, like her, we could nurture, love, and care for all the things and people we encounter. She gave us the qualities that would help us find our true nature, our spirit, our identity. She gave us the bridge to our heart.

"The stem of the pipe represents the spirit of the man. It is fashioned from wood to represent things that grow because, unlike the female, men cannot nurture a life until it is ready to emerge into the world. Their function is to guide, direct, protect, sustain, and enhance that life when it arrives—to help it grow. From the man we get strength, perseverance, fortitude, truth, loyalty, and respect so that like a man we can come to comprehend, understand, love, and care for all things we encounter. The man gives us the qualities to elevate our consciousness—our 'way of seeing'—about where we are. He gives us the bridge to our mind.

"To live a good life, to be 'good-hearted'—or *Midewewin* as our Ojibway Medicine Society is called—means we need to use both sets of gifts. Whether we are male or female we need to learn to live by our heart *and* live by our mind. When we learn to do this we are 'in balance.' The pipe represents that balance.

"When the male joins the female it's a very sacred union. Life is created. Another spirit is invited to come out onto the Earth and become the best it can become. Our future as human beings is more enriched, more whole, more sacred by this Creation. It is a very sacred union."

I sat on the living room floor for a long time while John went off to finish packing for his trip. It was mind-boggling. I felt incapable of understanding these teachings, much less living them. I walked away from his house that day with a lot of questions, mostly about myself and my ability to follow through.

All the teachings tumbled through my mind and I was astonished at how much had already escaped me. I shook my head and wondered what might have become of my life if I'd only chosen to come back to them as John suggested. My head ached with the flow of ideas and memories. There was much to consider and reconsider once I got back to my life in the city. Much to remember and recall. Much to relearn. I closed my eyes and soon fell fast asleep.

When I woke up John was there.

"Wha-wha!" he exclaimed. "You sleep pretty heavy. Must feel kinda safe out here, then, eh?"

I rubbed my eyes to clear them, glad that he was there. "Safe enough, I guess," I said and grinned.

"Well, you did it," he said. "You did your Vision Quest."

I was speechless. "My Vision Quest?" was all I could muster.

He handed me a small piece of bread and some water. "Eat this. Slowly, though. Really chew it, then wash it down with the water. You have to break your stomach back in slowly.

"That's what they call this thing you've done here: a Vision Quest. You're supposed to see your life, your purpose, your calling, your destiny. At least that's what they say so they can sell books and movies and stuff."

"Well, what am I supposed to see?"

He smiled. "Whatever," he said.

"Whatever?"

"Yeah. Whatever. Did you see anything up here at all?" he asked.

"I saw lots," I said.

"Like?"

"Like lots of things," I replied and began to tell him about every event of the last three nights. He listened carefully and said nothing to interrupt me until I had finished.

Then he said: "Lots of people nowadays really want things to be romantic. They want this way of ours to be all magical and mystical and mysterious. They want to come out on a Vision Quest and see something really amazing.

Something that knocks their socks off and makes for really good telling, sells books, makes them a shaman or a teacher or a healer, medicine man, medicine woman. You know, things like bears and wolverines, wolves and mountain lions visiting them and turning into old men or old women right in front of them and telling them great secrets about our way. They want the whole Hollywood thing. Like anything less isn't worth a damn, not believable, or somehow less Indian. They think that's how it's supposed to be.

"You're supposed to have a vision, but it's not meant to be a big production number. Oh, some people have them, that's a fact, and those people are very fortunate, very blessed to connect with the spirit world like that. But most of us are just Indians, just Ojibways, just Cree, English, Scots, French, or whatever. Just people. Our visions are less startling but just as powerful. We're supposed to see *ourselves*. And our place in the world. We're supposed to see the people we'd most like to be and the people we have been up to this point. And you know, when you see that, you've really seen something special, because most people never even take the time to look. You took four days out of your life. You took four days without water, food, or shelter. You took four days completely unarmed with the things we all like to arm ourselves with these days: possessions, property, all kinds of things. All the things we lose ourselves in. You came out here unarmed and unadorned and let the world have its way with you. And you saw something."

And I did. I had seen myself. The dream was my vision. I'd seen myself in all my pain, confusion, isolation, and deprivation. I had seen the trail I had followed, the one that had led me to that hill, that morning, that teaching. I told him about the dream.

"The dream," I said. "That's what I was supposed to see."

"Well, yes and no," John said. "You kinda had to be able to see your life to understand it, but mostly you had to see that you can be safe on this land, that you are a part of it, that it's a part of you, that you belong, that you always did. That's your vision. The dream is a gift. Extra. It's a teaching."

"What do you mean?"

"Well, the colours of the blanket for one thing. Purple is the colour that represents spirituality in our way. Orange is the colour that represents the old teachings. There's a teaching in that," he said.

"What is it?"

He laughed. "Always want the Shake 'n' Bake answer, don't you? Well, the truth is that it's your duty to find out for yourself what it means. You have to spend time going back to that dream, to learn what it's saying to you. But the good thing is that it's yours. No one else owns that dream; no one else is supposed to learn what you're supposed to learn from it. Kinda like you've got your own textbook now."

I finished the bread and water slowly. I felt slightly irritated. I'd expected to end this ordeal with a handful of answers. Now, four days later, all I had was a handful more questions. I wondered about that, wondered whether this "being Indian" thing was always going to be a search, always another ordeal.

"So is that it?" I asked finally.

"Not quite," John said.

"Not quite? What do you mean 'not quite?'"

"You need to do one more thing before we head back to the city—one more thing to complete this journey."

With that he stood up and beckoned me to follow him. We headed off into the bush beyond the hill and began to walk.

It was sunny, bright and warm. We walked and talked for miles. John pointed out the birds and small animals we passed, called each of them by their Ojibway names and told me stories about them.

Finally, we stopped at the edge of a small meadow. It was beautiful. The wind played amongst the branches of the highest trees and chased the tops of the grasses like a game. The sun painted large patches of shadow in the forest. There wasn't a sound to be heard. John and I stood very quietly drinking in the sight. After a while he took a great, deep breath, looked at me, smiled, and said, "Lots going on here, isn't there?"

I didn't know what he meant. To me the meadow was just a peaceful little place in the mountains. As hard as I tried I couldn't see any of the action he suggested was taking place.

"What do you mean?" I asked finally.

Again, he smiled. "Well," he said, "sometimes your eyes don't tell you the truth in what's around you. The most important things are hidden and sometimes you have to learn to see all over again."

I still didn't know what he meant and he could tell that this bothered me. "Sit here," he said, pointing to a log lying in the grass. "Sit here and look around you. Try to see what's going on. Look really hard. When you think you see it, come back to the hill and tell me."

Then he walked back into the forest and disappeared. I sat on the log and strained to see this activity that John saw. I saw the grasses and leaves sway with the wind. I saw a few ants struggle past my feet. Now and then a small bird flitted amongst the bushes, and chipmunks sounded their displeasure when a bird got too close to their supply of seeds or nuts. The shadows moved slightly as time passed, but to my eyes there was nothing, no goings-on like John saw.

But I knew he wouldn't have asked me to stay if there wasn't something to see. So I concentrated harder. With all my willpower I fought to see something, anything. But there was nothing but a quiet meadow in the mountains. Soon, I began to feel angry at myself, then sad because I couldn't see what he wanted me to see. Again I thought I had failed. After four days of discomfort and agony, of trying very hard to discover what it meant to be an Indian, a Native, it saddened me and hurt me that I couldn't understand. The Vision Quest hadn't worked, I told myself. It obviously hadn't worked because I was totally unable to see what John intended me to see. I had no vision. I had no clue.

I closed my eyes. I breathed very deeply and slowly. I allowed myself to feel everything I was feeling, and when I felt calm I opened my eyes again.

It was the same meadow. But instead of struggling to see, I felt peaceful. I relaxed. I began to feel at home sitting on that small log on the grass and the more comfortable I became the more closely I was able to look at things. I saw hundreds of varieties of plants, dozens of kinds of trees and rocks, mosses, mushrooms, and scores of bugs moving here and there. I smiled. There *was* a lot going on when you really looked, but something told me that John had meant me to see even more. So I relaxed and let myself sink deeper and deeper into the feeling of being a part of all that was around me. When I finally walked back to the hill I was smiling, filled with the joy of discovering a great secret—a secret I couldn't wait to share.

John was busy sitting on the ledge and carving a block of wood. When he saw me he smiled. "Looks like you saw something," he said.

"Yes," I told him. "You were right. There *is* lots going on out there."

"For example?" he asked.

"There was a tree," I said. "A big pine tree. It was really tall and strong. And old, like a grandfather. It stood there all proud because it had survived a lot of winters and lightning and floods. But it was really quiet, too—humble, happy just to be a part of the forest. I looked at it for the longest time, let my eyes really see it—every branch, from the top right down to the bottom.

"And there, close to where its trunk went into the earth, was a tiny seedling. It was only about four inches tall, small and beautiful. The more I looked at that tiny tree the more I saw what was going on," I explained.

John looked at me as if I was the teacher now. "Go on," he said.

"Well, that little seedling was growing up in the shadow of that big, old pine tree. At first I didn't think it had a chance because the big tree would use up all the moisture the seedling needed to grow. But then I saw that this wasn't happening at all. As I watched, the wind made the branches of the big tree move, and when they did the little tree was covered in sunlight. It was really hot out there and I realized that the big tree was *protecting* the little one. Too much sun would kill it, and the grandfather tree was giving it just enough shade and just enough sun so it would grow.

"Then I saw more. The trunk of the grandfather tree was sheltering the little one from big winds that might snap it or tear it from the ground. When it rained, the waters would be filtered through the branches of the big tree and land softly on the seedling instead of washing it away. When winter came, the trunk would keep the snow from piling on top of the seedling and crushing it. And the roots of the big tree made the soil around the seedling firm so that its own roots could sink deep into firm soil and it would be safe as it grew.

"I could see that little tree as it grew, protected and safe in the shelter of that big, old pine. It got stronger and stronger as it grew and that old pine allowed it to find its own place in the forest. Eventually, I could see that seedling become a proud but humble old tree itself, needing less and less of the grandfather tree's protection.

"Then there would come a time when that grandfather tree needed to go back to the earth that it grew from. When that time came, instead of letting it just fall and crash to earth, that seedling would be strong enough, humble enough, to let the grandfather fall through its branches, slowing its fall and letting it settle to the ground peacefully, gracefully. In this way it would honour the old tree for everything it had given it as it grew. That seedling grew to be tall and strong because of what the old tree had given it.

"But then I saw something else. When that old tree had settled on the forest floor and gradually given itself back to the Earth, a new little tree sprang up from its body and began to grow in the protection and shelter of the big tree again.

"That's what I saw happening in that meadow. So you're right, John, there is a whole lot going on out there."

John just looked at me, nodded his head and put an arm around my shoulder. He never told me whether I was right or wrong, never questioned what I'd seen, but I could tell he was happy with my answer. We walked slowly down the hill after that. He told a few jokes, we laughed, and I felt stronger somehow, cleaner. I thought about the Vision Quest and how it had always sounded so much more dramatic than it had been for me. All the Hollywood images went through my head and I laughed.

"What's so funny?" John asked.

"Me," I said.

"Well, that's true enough, but what's funny right now?"

"I was thinking about how I always used to think about this Vision Quest thing. About how magical and mysterious it was supposed to be. It's the way I thought about all Indian things, I suppose. All thunder and lightning, shape-shifting, spells, magic, mystery. And it's not like that at all," I said.

"No," John replied slowly, "it's not. It's pretty simple, really. It's just that we human beings wanna be rewarded with a Technicolor dream instead of a black-and-white reality.

"Like the Vision Quest. For most of us, the reward is clarity—being able to see clearly. Our quest, our search, for vision is a search for clarity, and the ceremony is intended especially for that. When you remove all the things of the world that we human beings hide behind, you're left with only yourself, and when you put yourself, unarmed and unadorned, in the pure, unrelenting face of the world you can't help but see yourself as you really are. That's *vision*," he said.

I understood. With the understanding came the

knowledge of what I was to do with the tobacco pouches. While John waited I walked out alone into the forest and found that grand old tree. Kneeling at its base I offered a prayer of gratitude for the clarity I'd been graced with and then I hung that string of tobacco pouches from the highest branch I could reach. Giving those prayers back to the land felt right. I believed that all of the elements of my vision had come from the land itself and that it was only right to return them.

When I told him what I'd done John just smiled and tousled my hair. We got into the car to start our journey back to our regular lives.

"Can you tell me three things that you learned up there?" John asked.

I thought about it as he drove. Now that we were headed for a meal, a good shower, and a warm bed it hardly felt like I'd been gone at all. The tiny bit of bread and water I'd taken had filled me for now and lessened the ordeal in my mind. Still, it had been a powerful four days. I thought a long time and when we finally crested the last hill before the land fell away into the linear morass of the city I found the words.

"Most of all, I guess, being out there with nothing but a blanket and a canteen taught me to always be grateful for what I have and not resentful, angry, or hurt over what I don't have."

"That's good," John said. "That's a strong teaching."

"Yeah. I guess I saw that when I'm grateful for the things in my life I can learn to live with simplicity—a humble way of being. I can learn to live as if I were on a hilltop with a blanket, grateful for its warmth."

He nodded.

"Then, I guess, I learned that I need to learn how to choose peace over everything."

"Wow," John said. "That's big. Can you tell me more?"

"Well, when the ants came I wanted to swat at them and kill them at first, before I just let them have their way. All of us surviving taught me to respect life and that I only really have two choices in life: to live in peace or to live in conflict, in harmony or out of balance. The kind of peace I knew on the hill always results in growth, in more knowledge. Conflict, like the way I lived my life, always results in hurt or harm to ourselves and others."

He reached over and tousled my hair with one hand. When he looked at me there was a glisten of tears in his eyes.

"What else?" he asked.

"To give away what I most want to get," I said.

"What do you mean?"

"Well, if I want love, security, trust, friendship, and all those good things in life, then I need to give away those things to the people around me. *All* people, all the time. Not just Native people, but all people."

John nodded and heaved a huge sigh. Then he looked at me and smiled. He didn't need to say anything; I knew what he was feeling. By the time we pulled up to the front door of my apartment building I was glad to be back in the civilized world.

"You did well. I'm proud of you," he said, giving me a big hug.

"I'm proud of me, too," I said.

"It shows," he said and got into his car.

Watching him drive away I offered a small, unselfconscious prayer to Creation in thanks for the Vision Quest, for the teachings, and for John. I walked back into my life renewed and filled with a greater hope than I'd ever carried before.

*for* JOSHUA

*Ochiichagwe'Babigo'Ining Ojibway Nation*
*April 2002*

This land I walk upon is our land. When this reserve was created there was a Wagamese on the first band list. I can count back five generations, back to my great-grandmother, your great-great grandmother's time, and hear stories of her life and the lives of our relations from those who can still remember. This has always been our land and coming back here, walking here, feeling that history in the soles of my feet is a return for which there is no word in either Ojibway or English. "Profound" comes close, as does "spiritual." "Empowering" even flirts with the definition, but there's really no word to capture this essence. It's a feeling. It's home.

Your Uncle Charles showed me a trail through the bush. It meanders along the Winnipeg River a while then splits in two, with one path continuing along the river and the other curling back through the trees and rock to the head of the gravel road. There are otters here. Wolves have been seen, and eagles are frequent visitors at this time of year. Standing out on a point of land upstream from the near rapids, knee deep in snow, sunlight exploding like a flare off the ice, and Keewatin, the North Wind, freezing my face, I can see them. They are everywhere out here. Our family.

I see them scraping hides, smoking fish, setting traps and snares, fishing, picking berries, harvesting rice, and stalking moose and deer against the spattered canvas of autumn. I see them in their tents, a pot-bellied wood-stove pipe angled out the top, spruce boughs piled three feet deep on the floor to keep out the frost, and a huge teapot burbling away on the top of the stove. They're laughing, telling stories, mending nets, making snowshoes, or just sitting comfortably while that same North Wind blows icily across the landscape.

They're not really there, of course. It's just a stubborn particular of love, even hope, that allows me a glimpse at the life that resulted in us—you and me, my son. We are the sum of all of that and we are blessed to have sprung from it. In our blood flows the fortitude that saw them through harsh winters, the humility that allowed them to share all that the land provided, the grace that saw them through drought, flood, and famine, and the staunch iron will that held up against the unimaginable onslaught of settlement, development, disease, poverty, and alcohol. Our hearts, minds, and spirits are a measure of all that they endured. They are in us, just as surely as my booted feet are planted on this point of land, seeing them as they were, as they are today, and as they always will be. A people, strong and purposeful.

Coming here, to the sheltering arms of family, is the closing of a circle, a journey ending where it began. Home.

I want to be able to tell you that I came off that hill outside of Calgary and my life changed completely. I want to be able to tell you that seeing myself as I was in the years before that Vision Quest allowed me to travel beyond the fear, guilt, and shame that had bound me all my life. I want to be able to tell you that I healed, grew, and evolved into a strong, proud man—a warrior. I want to be able to tell you that I never drank again.

But I can't.

Fear is a hard foe to conquer. It's insidious. Fear is cunning and it eats away at you from the inside where you can't see it, where it can hide and work its sly damage to your spirit. I didn't conquer it on that hill. I only found out that I had it, that I had carried it forever. And that realization wasn't enough to heal me.

Sure, my life changed after that Vision Quest. It changed dramatically. Under John's direction I found more teachers, went to more ceremonies, learned more about the things in this world that we've come to call culture. And I became more and more Indian. Or at least I thought I did. But I still only learned these things in my head. I still only really committed them to memory and not to action. I didn't change. I looked the part—in fact, I took great pains to surround myself with the stuff of native life. I had rattles, hand drums, medicine shields, eagle feathers, artwork, carvings, and the sacred medicines around me all the time. But that was to dress up the outside, so that other people who looked at me and how I was living could think, "He's a real Indian." But like the person I was before the Vision Quest, I still lived in other peoples' heads and still made my choices based on what I thought they were thinking. I was still afraid to be me. I still didn't know what that meant.

I became a writer. The Creator blessed me with the ability to put words on paper, or cast them into the air with a microphone, and I was successful. Thousands of people across the country read my words. Thousands more heard me on the radio or saw the television programs I hosted and helped produce. Then, in 1991, I was given the honour of winning a National Newspaper Award for the Native issues columns I wrote for the *Calgary Herald* each week. The plaque had a line on it that read "Whose work is judged the best in the country." *The best in the country.* Me, a Grade 9–educated ex-convict, who made "runs" for winos, slept under bridges, stole, defrauded and bilked people, had never held the same job for a year, couldn't maintain a relationship with a woman or a friend, was suddenly judged "the best in the country" by a panel of experts.

I should have been honoured. But all I felt after I received that award was fear. I was afraid someone was going to find out about me. That I now had one more standard I could fail to live up to. That I wasn't a journalist. I wasn't a writer. I wasn't a success. I was just a fluke, a fraud, a liar. And at the root of those fears was the one overwhelming fear I'd carried all my life: that they'd find out there was something wrong with me, that I was unlovable and unworthy and they'd reject and abandon me.

And so I drank.

I drank because it felt better to pull the rug from under my own feet than run the risk of having someone else do it for me. I drank because I didn't believe I deserved the success I was having. I drank because I was afraid I couldn't maintain that success. I drank because rebuilding my life, starting over, was easier than keeping it going. I drank because alcohol always did for me what it had done the very first time, and that was to help me not to feel the feelings I carried.

And I drank out of guilt. John had introduced to me a way of being that was authentic, vibrant, and empowering. The more I absorbed of that way, the more I respected it. But when I drank again I felt guilty because I was disrespecting those teachings, I was dishonouring them, I was, as a friend once put it to me, "spitting in the Creator's face, knowing what you know and doing what you do." When I sobered up again, as I always did for short periods, I carried around a big pile of guilt over that dishonour. So guilt became my constant companion, too.

I became desperate. I needed more success in order to feel adequate, to place myself above the guilt and fear. So I worked. I worked hard. The reward of all that work was that I became "known" as a writer and I published my first book in 1994. Then I got drunk. For the next six years I achieved, then followed that achievement with a binge.

*Always.* Two more books appeared in stores. I taught at a university. I was a guest speaker at other universities. And I had a beautiful baby boy to carry my name: Joshua Richard Wagamese. But none of this was enough to quell the guilt and fear I felt in my gut. For six arduous years I stood up and fell down, stood up and fell down. And I re-created all the ordeals of my youth.

In that time I was sent to jail, lived on the street, went to detox, got beaten up, wandered from woman to woman, woke up on riverbanks, in dumpsters, back alleys, and strangers' homes. I cheated, lied, and stole. And always, always, I would get sober long enough to convince myself and the people around me that I was okay this time, that it would be different. But it never was.

Then one day I woke up on a riverbank and I wanted to die. I couldn't stand the thought of another day in the misery of my life. I looked at the water flowing past me and I thought that if I filled my pockets with enough rocks I could end this seemingly endless cycle of injury and disappointment for myself and others. I could quit being a victim—and victimizing others. I could check out and no one would miss me. I wanted to die so badly it seemed like a logical choice.

But the drinker in me needed one more bottle.

As it turns out, the Creator needed me to go off on a search for one more bottle. I found it, although I had no money. When you drink out of desperation you can always find a drink. That's the paradox of being a drunk like I was: even though the thing you need to feel better is actually killing you, you can always find it. Always. I found it with a group of desperate drinkers like myself and as we huddled under a railroad bridge, taking turns gulping down that whisky, I still had one eye on that river. Later, walking aimlessly about on my own, I lifted a bottle of mouthwash from a corner store and gulped it down as I stood in the middle of a bridge over that water. I was convinced it was finished, that I was finished, that I had no strength left for one more try.

But I was wrong.

I wound up in the hospital that day. I wound up connected to heart monitors and IVs dripping sufficient medication to allay the alcoholic seizures that were certain to follow. I was there five days. While I lay in that bed I had nothing to do but think. I thought about my life and how I had lived it.

I thought about John and how, when he died suddenly, I felt abandoned and utterly alone. Year after year I allowed memory to take me where it would and I watched myself slowly disappear despite the show I was putting on for the outside world. So many unnecessary losses, so many needless hurts inflicted and endured, so many wrong turns, so many excuses and denials. Sometime during the course of those four nights in that hospital bed I became convinced that I could do what John had asked me to start doing on that hill so long ago: to accept who I was.

I had another Vision Quest in detox. I admitted that I was a drunk and that, in the condition I was in on that hospital bed, I was hopeless. I was defeated. That if I drank again I would die—with or without rocks in the pocket.

I found people who were just like me and I began to travel with them. Over time they showed me exactly what John had shown me, that I wasn't bad, deficient, or unworthy—I was just a drunk who needed to stay sober in order to help himself. If I chose to do that, they offered to help me clean up the mess of my past and learn to use it as a tool for building a better future. Nothing was required but an earnest desire, and by the time I had been with them a month or so I had that desire.

The wonderful thing about that is that these were not Native people. Or at least, not all of them were. They were people who had lived with the same feelings about themselves that I had. They were just people. Just drunks who didn't drink, and they loved me until I could learn to love myself. With their help, I reconnected to the teachings John had introduced to me. I began to appreciate myself for surviving all I had put myself through and I found my way back to acceptance of who I was created to be. They helped me remember the most basic of our teachings: that we are gifted with our identities, and nothing is big enough to take that gift away from us. Ever. I was created to be a male Ojibway human being and those people helped me back to that recognition. They helped me back to learning how to honour it.

When I had been around them a long time and had investigated my life and shared it with people, something strange happened. I was walking down the street towards the library on a cold, grey morning, looking at the sky and thinking how magical life can be and how many benefits were being paid me for the work I had done on healing my hurts and wounds. I remembered that on the morning of my last drink, the sky had looked just as it did on the street that moment. I thought about that morning. And it hit me. All of a sudden it just dawned on me and I smiled— because it didn't hurt anymore. My life was no longer a Technicolor nightmare. It was a black-and-white reality. A reality that didn't hurt anymore.

And so I began to look at my Native life in the same way I'd looked at my drunkard's life. I searched my past and admitted where I had been wrong. I investigated myself and found lots to toss away. And, consequently, a lot to keep and rebuild my life around. I found the me that existed under the rubble of all I'd caused to collapse. I found beliefs and values I never knew I had. I found understandings I never recalled being given. I found a peace in being a male Ojibway human being that I never knew was possible. I just needed an earnest desire to learn and it had been granted me.

What I learned on that search is what I need to tell you, my son. I need to tell you because there are many places where I fell, and by telling you I might help you avoid them. That's my duty, my responsibility, and my honour.

For a long time our people have called this country home. This is where we fit, where we belong, and it is from here that our teachings sprang. We are who we are because of this land. When we stand upon it, even now, even with all of the changes that have scarred it, marred it, and made it less pure, we can feel the eternal connection that exists for us when our hearts are open. The sense of oneness that happens, the feeling of connection, is a result of hearts in tune with the land—resonating with each change, thrumming with the energy of its ongoing creation, tingling with expectancy at the wonders of each new season and beating with the measured, eternal rhythm of the drum at the centre of all of it. That's what makes us Ojibway people: the knowledge that the land is a feeling, and sensing it in the soles of our feet.

When we travelled about in the days long past, it wasn't a search for permanence that drove us. For the one place on the land that we could call ours. It wasn't a search for a territory we could control. It was for the *experience* of the land. We were bands of wanderers, perfectly at home wherever we were, at peace with the land and seeking an ever deeper relationship with it. Our travels gave us new perspectives, new ways of seeing, new teachings and a renewed sense of ourselves. The more we experienced of the land, the more we experienced ourselves. That's not in any book, it's not taught in any school, and there are a lot of people who will argue that we were just aimless, trying to scrounge survival from the land. But our people knew that we are who we are *because of* the land, and only through experience combined with teachings could we gain true knowledge. So we travelled. We experienced.

The cultural teachings of our elders, the tools of the pipe and drum and ceremony, are all meant to help us get back to belief in who we are. They are meant to centre us, to take us right back to our hearts. To the truth of us. When we get there, we discover that the tools are merely aids, and that what really matters is what we carry in our hearts.

I was confused for a long time, lost in pride, and I started to think about Canada as a nation. And that meant history. History told me that our people got a raw deal. It told me that we had had our land stolen from us. It told me that we had suffered through the tearing away of our culture, languages, and ceremonies. It told me that we had become second-class citizens on the land that once belonged to us. All I could see was that the settlers cared only for themselves. They were greedy and self-centred and could only see our people as a problem to be solved. Because of that we have suffered great injustices and hurts and someone had to be responsible for fixing things. Until that happened we had no choice but to be separate, to stand to one side and demand our due. That was how I saw Canada.

But Canada is not a nation first. It is people. It is the feeling of the land. And it's the feeling of the people on the land *for* the land. That's what defines this country: the feeling of the people for the land. Not only those of us who were here first, who are native to it, but everyone. There aren't many people in any part of Canada that don't love the country for itself. You won't have to travel far to find people who love it for the plains, the mountains, the muskeg, lakes, rivers, marshes, tidal bores, glaciers, estuaries, deltas, and seas. All my travelling had taught me that. So had the people I'd met.

Earl loved rivers and he built his life on the banks of one. It cradled him, wrapped him up in it its sights and sounds and smells. The coal miner's sons from Sydney loved the smells and textures of harbour life and made them come alive in their music. Sylvie and Luc carried the rustic joy of the Québec bush to the campus of a university. Glen, the rambler, adored the feisty, beer-swilling rollick of the bush camps, sawmills, and mines because they all reflected the land on which they were made—a bold, swaggering land—and he lived his life with the same verve and swagger. The Saskatchewan farmer's son and the Métis steelworker were filled with the ache and passion of a prairie life, and their lives were poems and paeans to it. All of their stories came from the experience of generations spent on the land. They came from heartache and loss, disillusionment and sorrow, success and celebration, birth and dying—the same places our stories come from. That night around the fire in Nipigon had taught me this, had placed all of it in my soul. It took sitting on that hill and thinking about unity and belonging to bring it back.

You don't have to be Ojibway, Cree, Haida, Inuk, or Blackfoot to love Canada. You don't have to be Native, because the truth is that everyone born here is native to this land. Everyone who has ever laid a loved one to rest within the breast of this earth has a spiritual tie to it that is as strong, as valid, as our own. Everyone who can trace a line to ancestors here, everyone whose lives have sprung from a relationship with the land, everyone whose family story is one that includes hardship, struggle, and a reclaimed dignity, has a right to claim themselves as native to Canada. We are the *original people* of this land, and that will never change, but everyone whose first breath is from the crystal clear air of Canada is native to this country. There are many people among us who will be angered by that thought, many who will deny it, but if history, intention, and responsibility have anything at all to teach us about ourselves, it is that our thinking must change.

We are the original people. We are the ones who emerged from the forest to welcome the strangers when they arrived here so long ago. We are the ones who saw them suffer from the harshness of life on the land. We are the ones who came to their aid. We are the ones who guided them through seemingly impossible territories to show them the splendour of the country. We are the ones who taught them to respect it for its power. We are the ones who showed them how to nurture it, to gather its resources, to reap its blessings, and to honour it for them. We taught them to survive here. We taught them to grow. We taught them to take this land like a potion, to drink it deeply into themselves, to feel its energy, its transforming juices, and to become more. We taught them to be at home here. We taught them how to love this country.

It was our role to do those things. It was our responsibility. It was the original instructions handed from Creator to us—to walk gently upon the land and do each other no harm. It is still our role. It is still our responsibility.

As original people we are the guardians of the land. Protectors. That role will never change. When you protect something you keep it from harm. You cradle it within your spirit, and nurture it in everything you do so that it will grow, become more, become what the Creator intended. We cannot know what the Creator intends for anything. Even with our own children we do not know. But we have to follow the rules of protectors nonetheless and nurture them. Tecumseh's mother did not know what the Creator intended when he was crawling around her wigwam. Big Bear's mother did not know. Neither did the mothers of Sacajawea or Pocahontas. They protected them, guided them, nurtured them, kept them from harm and they became *great*. It remains for us to do the same with Canada. Always. Because we do not know what the Creator intends for it. That will come to pass in the Creator's time. But we know what he intends for us and that is to be this land's guardians—to show the way.

As original people we know how to honour this land. We know how to bless it. We know how to approach it spiritually. We know how to take the lessons from that spirituality and give it back to the land.

The truth is, Joshua, that a real Indian is a person who lives feeling. Real Indians use the teaching tools of our way to travel inside themselves. Real Indians, having made that sacred journey, discover their own truth—their selves. When they discover their selves they discover that the Creator has graced them with another tremendous gift: the gift of choice.

When you know who you are you can choose anything. You can choose what to wear, where to live, where to work, what to study, the activities you enjoy, the people you want for friends. Everything. You can choose everything that the world has to offer and it will not change the fact of who you are. You can experiment with choice. You can try anything on for size, and if it fits and you're comfortable, keep it, make it your own. Or, on the other hand, if it feels cumbersome and awkward, you can let it go and make another choice. Armed with identity, the knowing, you are empowered with choice to help make that knowing an ongoing thing. You can always learn more about who you are. You can always become more and more real.

That's the truth of our way.

As parents and teachers we need to tell our children this—that you can never be less than who you were created to be. You never have to qualify. You never have to prove yourself. You just need to *be*.

Each of us carries within ourselves the memory of drums on distant hills. In each beat of our hearts we hear the wails and chants of singers, of dancers' shuffling steps, of spirits raised in one great voice to praise the Earth and the breadth of her dominion. In our veins runs the blood of generations past, and in that rich, thick flow are tribal memories of days long gone when our people truly lived in union with the land. Those memories flicker and dance with every move we make in this modern world. They call to us. Beckon to us in dream time. Rise up like sudden phantoms in times of trouble. Ebb and flow like tidal waters in the casual day-in day-out routines of living. They are in our blood, and our spirits long to be reconnected to them. We all crave, as deeply as any thirst, a return to those tribal fires where the people gathered in one small band to huddle against the night. A return to times when we lived in harmony, balance, brotherhood, and belonging. A return to the shelter of those tribal flames, to the sense of warmth they gave, the belief that in that one small circle of our people could be found the hearts and bones of our survival. We've felt that fire slowly die in our communities. We've watched its light fade, its warmth disperse, and its embers lose their spark.

And that is what we mourn.

From that mourning comes a staunch desire. A desire to re-create it all. To rebuild it. To live as our tribal hearts would have us live—in unity, peace, and brotherhood. That is what our tribal hearts desire and that is what we miss.

We go to great lengths sometimes to make it real for ourselves. We go to great lengths to fan those dying embers, to stoke those flames back to life, to chase away the night. In our cultural lives we insist that real Indians know how to sing and dance and drum. In our traditional lives we insist that real Indians attend every ceremony, make every offering, possess all the medicines, and speak our languages. In our communities we insist that real Indians live as everyone else lives, choose what everyone else chooses, and fit in by being exactly the same. We insist on all of this because we have seen how quickly things can disappear into the night and we need everyone to fan the dying embers of those tribal fires. We don't want to lose any more of ourselves, so we get tough on each other, demand that we all be what we believe everyone needs to be to stay strong, to live, to survive. We don't want to grieve the loss of another part of ourselves.

Our neighbours in this country need to hear this, too. They need to hear that there is so much unrest among their Native brothers and sisters because of grief and longing. They seek to understand us, but we have too often closed the door to our lodges and said that only Indians may come in. They wonder why we seem so upset, why we insist on land claims, special treaty rights, a voice in political decisions that affect us. They wonder why we are so angry at them.

In truth, we're not angry. We're sad. They need to know this. They need to know that for us, for tribal people who carry the memories of drums on distant hills, the land itself haunts us. It reminds us of what we have lost every time we look upon it. It reminds us how far away from those tribal fires we have moved, of how incredibly things have changed, of how with every fibre of our beings we seek a return to the things that kept us vital, dynamic, spiritual, and alive forever. They need to know that every land claim, treaty negotiation, blockade, and court case is born out of that desire. They are born out of a spiritual hunger, not a physical greed. They are actions created by a profound sadness and longing for the flames of those old tribal fires. For a sense of who we are. For an image of ourselves cast in the light of traditional fires. They need to know that they are actions taken to ensure that we will not need to grieve the loss of another part of ourselves.

If they can understand this, they can understand us, because everyone has lost someone or something they miss with a longing that is deep and blue and cold. So it is with us, and we need to tell them that.

This is why it is so hard to be considered a real Indian in this world—because it's easier to calm someone's anger than it is to heal someone's sadness or to fill a lonely need. It's only natural, I suppose, for someone carrying the crushing inner burden of loneliness to do whatever it takes to make it go away. At least that was true for me. When our people tell each other that they need to do this, they need to act this way, they need to wear this, to be seen here or seen there, they are speaking from that loneliness. They are trying to recreate that tribal life today, trying to rebuild it, make it vital and alive again.

But the secret is that we can never bring back those days. We can never recreate the buffalo hunt. The world has changed far too much. But if we recognize the loneliness we carry and own it, call it ours, then what we can do as a people is to recreate and carry the *spirit* of those things in our hearts. We may not relight the fires that used to burn in our villages, but we can carry the embers from those fires in our hearts and learn to light new fires in a new world. We can recreate the spirit of community we had, of kinship, or relationship to all things, of union with the land, harmony with the universe, balance in living, humility, honesty, truth, and wisdom in all of our dealings with each other.

I don't know when or if we will see each other. I don't know if you will ever read this book. But I hope so. I wrote it for you, and in the writing I began to realize that there were probably hundreds, maybe thousands of young Native people who might need to know this story, too. There are many who have been denied the presence of a father in their lives. Many who have never been offered the teachings this book talks of. Many who carry the same set of feelings about themselves that I once carried. Many who maybe already drink the way I drank to kill those feelings. And I just knew you would want to share this with them.

But, ultimately, it is yours.

The truth of my life today is threefold because I will always be three things in this world. First, I will always be a male, Ojibway human being. I always was. Secondly, I will always be a drunk who can never drink again. Lastly, I will always be your father. Nothing in the world can ever change that.

Seek me out when you are ready. I won't be too hard to find. I'll be on the land somewhere, feeling its heartbeat on the soles of my feet, knowing with each breath that it is home, that I am home, wherever I might be.

Until then, my son, I love you.

*Your father*

# ACKNOWLEDGEMENTS

I would like to thank the Canada Council for the Arts for its generous support in the creation of this manuscript. Also, my heartfelt gratitude goes to Chief Allan Luby and the Band Council of Ochiichagwe'Babigo'Ining First Nation for the space to complete it.

Thanks to my family, for their support and belief in me; my agent, Bruce Westwood, for friendship and guidance; Natasha Daneman, for enduring the phone calls, e-mails and nomadic movements; Maya Mavjee and Nick Massey-Garrison at Doubleday, for encouragement, advice and acceptance. Further, immense gratitude to Shelagh Rogers for her humanitarianism, Dawn Maracle, Drew Hayden-Taylor,

Carla Robinson, Sally Catto, Kika Mowry, Peter Simpson, Professor John Wadland, and all the friends of Bill W. for being there when I needed them.

And especially to Catherine, Sebastian, Pizhoo, and Buddy, for giving me a home and the strength to write this book.

# ABOUT THE AUTHOR

Richard Wagamese's award-winning first novel, *Keeper 'n Me*, helped establish him as one of Canada's major new literary talents. A former columnist for the *Calgary Herald*, he received a National Newspaper Award for his writing. Richard Wagamese lives in Ontario.